Karl Brandes

Rome and the Popes

Karl Brandes

Rome and the Popes

ISBN/EAN: 9783741189944

Manufactured in Europe, USA, Canada, Australia, Japa

Cover: Foto ©Lupo / pixelio.de

Manufactured and distributed by brebook publishing software (www.brebook.com)

Karl Brandes

Rome and the Popes

CONTENTS.

Translator's Preface		5
Preface of the Author		7

PART THE FIRST.

I.	—Introductory	23
II.	—The City at the Time of St. Peter's first Visit	26
III.	—St. Peter's Arrival in Rome	29
IV.	—The Apostle's Preaching	33
V.	—The early Christians of Rome	36
VI.	—The Chair of St. Peter	40
VII.	—The Persecution under Nero—St. Peter's Martyrdom	43
VIII.	—Peter the Visible Head of the Visible Church	48
IX.	—The true Church of Christ is Roman and Catholic	52
X.	—St. Peter in subterranean Rome	56
XI.	—The Christian Regeneration of the City,—the Paradox of History	61
XII.	—The Vatican	66
XIII.	—The Bronze Statue of St. Peter	70
XIV.	—The City of the Cæsars become the City of the Popes	74
XV.	—Rome the Centre of the Christian World	80
XVI.	—The Patrimony of St. Peter	84
XVII.	—The Successor of St. Peter become Protector of the City against the Byzantine Emperor and the Subalpine Barbarians	89
XVIII.	—Development of the Pope's Political Position into Sovereignty	94

XIX.—Rome as the Capital of the States of the Church 102
XX. —The Papal States in a new Phase 109
XXI.—The Papal States in their Relation to Italy...... 114
XXII.—The Saracens in Italy........................ 118

PART SECOND.

I. —Rome without Peter......................... 127
II. —Secularized Rome of the ninth Century 132
III. —Rome under the tyrannical Dynasties of the tenth Century 138
IV. —Nomination of the Popes by the German Kaiser. 143
V. —Italian Nationality 148
VI. —The Vatican and the Capitol.................. 155
VII. —The Popes at Avignon........................ 162
VIII.—The Ghost of ancient Paganism in the Ruins of Rome 166
IX. —Rome a Republic... 173
X. —The City without the Pope................... 179
XI. —The Roman Republic at the close of the XVIII. Century 184
XII. —Rome, Capital of the Tiber-department......... 188
XIII.—The Republic of Assassination................ 197
XIV.—The TWO HUNDRED AND FIFTY-EIGHTH PETER and his Rome 204

TRANSLATOR'S PREFACE.

On the first page of his preface, Dr. BRANDES briefly tells us that the object of this little volume is "to show the close relation, the inseparable union that exists between Rome and the See of Peter;" or, in other words, to prove that the supreme temporal power in Rome is annexed forever to the Papacy, so that the Pope shall be ruler in Rome, or, at least, that his influence in the government of that city shall be paramount, till Rome—till the world is no more. A bold thesis, unquestionably, in face of all that has taken place these last few years in Europe, and what is now going on in Italy.

All Catholics must undoubtedly wish that the Pope be in such a position of political independence as would leave him untrammeled by the interference of any secular power in the exercise of his spiritual authority. All Catholics had fain see him, too, in possession of such a revenue as would enable him to carry on with facility the vast administration of the universal Church. *Nearly* all Catholics have asserted that, to secure these two, it is morally necessary that the Pope should enjoy sovereign power in Rome. We said *"nearly* all Catholics;" for some few not only deny what the majority *have asserted*, but dare maintain that it is no longer even expedient that the Pope should retain the sovereignty of the States of the Church. This opinion, however, is singular and held only by some few singular and erratic individuals. How they reconcile it with Props. LXXV and LXXVI. of the late Encyclical we cannot imagine.

But whatever we may wish on the subject, there is no denying that the impression is becoming very general among all classes of Catholics, that the Pope has but a very short tenure of his temporal dominions. This belief is based on the assumption that there necessarily exists a direct antagonism between the Papal sovereignty and those principles of democracy which have become the ruling influence in modern society:—principles, which all admit are destined, for good or ill, to shape the future of Europe and European civilization.

But this is a mere assumption. Let Europe become democratic, rulers of some kind there must still be; and why the Pope should not be one of them, why he should not be able to rest his strength upon democracy as well as Napoleon or Victor Emanuel, we cannot comprehend. We can very easily comprehend, however, the Holy Father's detestation of wrongs committed now-a-days, in the name, but without the sanction, of democratic principles.

The question of the Pope's temporal power, Dr. BRANDES views from a stand-point, all his own. If it be God's will that the Pope should retain sovereign political independence in Rome, the "Revolution" will rage in vain. The sceptre did not pass from Juda till the time appointed in the decrees of heaven. Now, Dr. BRANDES undertakes to show in a rapid, but masterly glance at Roman history, that God has manifested in a thousand ways for the last fifteen hundred years His positive unaltered will that Rome should know no ruler save His own Vicar upon earth, the successor of St. Peter. The author does not deny that the Pope, for a season, may be deprived of his dominions. A Nabuchodonosor may arise, but he and his deeds shall perish, and God's designs will in the end be accomplished.

Dr. BRANDES' little volume may be styled a philosophico-historical essay. That nicety and precision which we should look for in the tame historian, it would be unjust to require of our author. He wrote for a passing occasion. His conviction of the truth of his thesis was strong. He was full of his subject, and thought rather of what he had to say than how it might best be said. Arguments here and there may not be put as fully and as forcibly as they might be. But this will not affect the one main argument of the book, the only thing which the learned and lamented Benedictine had at heart.

In our translation we have endeavored to imitate the style and spirit of the original. We have striven to give not only the matter but the manner of the author. How far we have succeeded it isnot ours to judge.

W. J. W.

SETON HALL, *October 24th*, 1867.

PREFACE OF THE AUTHOR.

This year the Church has celebrated the eighteenth centenary aniversary of St. Peter's Martyrdom. He died at Rome in the sixty-seventh year of the Christian era. The occasion we thought a fitting one to publish the following pages. Our object in writing them, was to show the close relation, the inseparable union, that exists between the see of Peter and Rome, the Queen city of the world. This union has lasted unbroken since the death of St. Peter. It will so last to the end of time. The revolutionists may shout "*Roma o la morte*," Rome or death, but, despite their frantic efforts, Rome shall still remain the city of St. Peter's successors, the city of the Popes.

It were not to be expected, that a work of this kind should be purely theological. In fact, theology can have but a very small share in it. History and political philosophy are to be chiefly dealt with. However, when questions of theology spontaneously spring up in the course of the work, we shall treat them as far as they come within the scope of our undertaking, without, however, allowing them to break off the general chain of argument.

Rome, the capital of the ancient world, was made by St. Peter, the capital of the modern Christian world. This is Rome's high prerogative, and one that no other city can ever dispute with her.

"Thou art Peter (a rock), and upon this rock I will build my Church, and the gates of hell shall not prevail against it." These are the words of the Redeemer. Peter was made the foundation of the Church. Peter's see became the foundation see of that Church. As the Church was not to fail, that see on which it rests, could not fail. Through Peter, the Saviour's words are derived to the see, to the city of Rome itself. They imply a stability in that see, a stability in which there is a deep significance not applicable in the case of any other.

For, although the received axiom be true, "*Ubi Petrus, ibi ecclesia*"—WHERE PETER IS, THERE IS THE CHURCH, nevertheless, in her normal condition, the Church requires some local centre, some fixed spot, where she may be visible in her visible head. That such, too, is the ordinance of God, there can be no doubt. His will is manifest in a thousand facts. The most superficial reader of history cannot but observe that, whenever he, who holds from Christ, as St. Peter's successor, the power to bind and to loose, was driven from that see divinely chosen for his residence, a deep commotion shook the world, a cataclysm came on, which all but shattered the entire fabric of civil society.

Political disturbances seldom or never entail the disastrous consequences that invariably follow religious ones. It is, besides, always much easier to allay the former than the latter. So closely however, are the two orders, the civil and the religious, intertwined, that disturbances can never occur in the one without exciting commotion in the other. Each acts on the other, and, say the mistaken politicians of the day what they will about separation of Church and state, each is still necessary to the other and will remain so.

When the unholy effort is now made to undermine that rock on which Christendom has for ages reposed, we may well tremble for the safety of civil society. It is reeling on the edge of a precipice, over which it may roll at any moment, and be shivered to atoms in the fall. The Church is conscious of the impending danger, and would fain avert it. But if it must come, if civil society must rush upon its own ruin, she is conscious, too, that mid the chaos and destruction that will ensue, she will still rest securely upon her rock, and appear, through all, living and indestructible, the one great enduring upholder of order in the human family. She saw the commencement of every dynasty, of every state, kingdom and empire, now on earth. She will also witness their end. She alone is perpetual.

Should society in its present form be destroyed and a new order of things arise, the Church will live on, through, and with, the new states, new dynasties, new laws, new rights, new titles that may come up; or rather, they will have to cling round her as babes round their mother for protection and support. All else may fail, but fail, the Church cannot. She shall last, for her's are those words of the Saviour: "BEHOLD, I AM WITH YOU ALL DAYS, EVEN TO THE CONSUMMATION OF THE WORLD." It is said of one of the Egyptian pyramids that it was built before the flood, and that it alone, of all things human, withstood the rush of the waters, and appeared uninjured when they subsided. So shall it be with the Church. She is firmly founded on the rock of Peter, and thereon maintained by the divine power. Should the storm which now gathers on the horizon burst over Europe and sweep away every vestige of civilization, the Church would still brave the might and the fury of the tempest and remain, like that Egyptian pyramid, when all else was gone. She is imperishable.

It is most remarkable, as it is undeniably true, that none of the great ones of the earth ever interfered with the Holy See, without suffering for the same. Sooner or later, the man who raised his hand against the successor of St. Peter, was sure to be overtaken by the marked vengeance of heaven.

The miserable wretches, who are barking like blood-hounds round that See to-day, will, we feel assured, have bitter cause ere they die, to repent their doings. Their besotted leader who makes so much ado about the Capitol, had better remember, as lately admonished by the majestic Pius IX., that should he ever get so far again, the Tarpean is close by. But Garibaldi's little day is done. The bullet of Aspromonte was hardly necessary to stop his course. He has already died a moral death. His own ranting killed him. The scrawls, he sends from time to time to the press, only serve to show the world how dead and gone he is. And he lives to see this — lives to see the dazzle of his spurious glory die out. The hero that was, is no more. Garibaldi, the hero, has been hurled from the Tarpean. Naught is left but the ignoble carcass. His very admirers are now beginning to be confounded at seeing their idol thus prostrate and powerless. They begin to see, too, which is more humiliating, that he never was but a dagon, that he really never did effect anything, save where treason led the way and left little to be done. So much for Garibaldi and his penalty. But the man who stirred up these wild elements, who hounded on these fanatics against God's Church under the vain delusion that he had power to repress them again at will, erred gravely and sinned deeply. The spirit he has evoked, he cannot allay. He would now say "thus far and no farther." But this, the language only of the Eternal. Mortal may not use it. It is said of king Tullus Hostilius, that, when of old he introduced these words into the augural rites of ancient Rome, he was on the instant smitten by lightning from Heaven. So in our own time was he, but yesterday so mighty, brought suddenly low for madly attempting to disturb that rock on which rests the Church of Christ. Would he might even now take heed! But does he even suspect wherefore this hath happened him? Perhaps not, and perhaps he will not, till the arm of God is laid more terribly and more visibly upon him, and the successor of St. Peter point him out and say "Thine is the crime"—*tu es ille vir*.

Between the Church and the world a life-and-death struggle is commenced. It is at bottom a conflict between barbarism and civilization, between godlessness and Christianity. It is very natural that the enemies of Christianity should direct their first efforts against the Church of Christ. It is natural, too, they should choose for their point of attack, that spot wherein she seems most defenseless. They dare not approach a strong clear dogma, wherein there could be no misconception. Their efforts would be fruitless. All Christendom would spring to arms against them. But owing to the artful, insidious manner in which the attack on Christianity is made, it is deeply to be regretted that many who love Christ and mean well by his Church, are unfortunately ranged, in this struggle, on the side of His and her enemies. They argue that the question is one of merely accidental connection with the Church; that it matters really very little whether the Pope retain or lose his temporal sovereignty. They think his independence can be safely secured without it, and in regard to the whole matter, different men have different plausible theories of their own. Some would wish to see him retain his dominions, but insist he must adopt a different constitution.

Then, there is this, that, and the other form of government that he might adopt. At all events, he must bring his principles into conformity with modern ideas and civilization. Now, this is all sheer nonsense. Adopt a constitution! Every body knows how unnatural a thing it is to frame and force a constitution upon a population. Constitutions, to work well, must naturally grow up from, and be developed out of the ideas, habits, manners, and prejudices of a people. Besides, as regards the States of the Church in particular, it must ever be borne in mind that the Pontifical government must exist under somewhat different circumstances, as it exists for a different end, from any other. Of its very nature, it is unique in the world, and cannot, in many points, resemble other administrations. Adopt a constitution! Now, what is the invariable effect of such a step? The foreign frame-work into which a population is thus violently crushed and squeezed, will inevitably choke up all the germs of civil life and liberty which were there in process of natural evolution. In the case of the Roman States, it would at once destroy the dominion of the Popes. The princely power in those states, on account of its annexed spiritual character, is necessarily elective. It is therefore devoid of all those means whereby hereditary monarchies secure strength and durability. This, of itself, renders it necessary that the Pope should stand towards his subjects in relations somewhat different from those of other rulers. But all that could be done towards remodeling his government and improving the condition of his states, has been done, and that most cheerfully, by Pius IX. Other governments, we know, have tried political changes. But what were they? Some could scarce count as many years of existence, as the pontifical government can centuries. Their existence had no significance, and their influence was little felt outside their own boundaries. If these went under in the transition, another government succeeded, and few, save the immediate inhabitants, were affected by the change. But quite different is it with the government of the States of the Church. This government was divinely raised up to fulfil a divine mission. For a thousand years and upwards, it has stood firm and unchangeable 'mid the many convulsions of European society. And should that government be now toppled over, what can be given us in its stead? What secret influence of law and order can be substituted for that of the independent Father of Christendom? An all important question, this, and let him who can, solve it. To disturb the foundations of society, to batter down, for a wild experiment, the columns on which it rests, is a crime of crimes. Yet such, the sin of our days. Against this, the successor of St. Peter has raised his voice; against this, both as Pope and prince, he is struggling,—as Pope resting securely on the divine foundation of the Church, and as prince fulfilling the high mission given him to perform towards Christendom, by defining the duties, the rights and privileges both of the governing and the governed.

And now as to the "progress of the age." The Church never was, never could be, and is not, opposed to real progress. She is though, and ever must be, opposed to that progress which but leads to destruction, and is only a step backwards towards a godless barbarism. Her natural and necessary action, both upon the individual and upon society, is that of a reformer. With regard to society, she abominates and condemns the pitiable antichristian legislation, which is being foisted upon it, and shows by the wisdom of her own laws, that she is the true reformer and friend of progress. Every page of those folios wherein her legislative enactments are recorded, and handed down from generation to generation for the guidance of mankind, is a monument of her love of progress. Pope John XXII., on occasion of his making a new collection of disciplinary laws, thus speaks: "On account of the mutability of man, no legislation excogitated by mortals, will be found to suit all times and circumstances."

The collections of ecclesiastical canons and decrees, are noble models of what legislation should be, and modern quacks might learn much therefrom for the public weal, did they only apply themselves to the study.

Considering the difference of circumstances, the same spirit of wisdom which pervades the general legislation of the Church, is also clearly discernible in that of the Papal States. On the latter, the personal views and character of the reigning pontiff, will, indeed, at times, leave their impression. But taking it as a whole, we cannot help being struck with the admirable uniformity of views and measures that has characterized that long line of rulers. No matter what their antecedents, no matter what their education or prejudices, no matter what their race, habits, tongue or country, on the subject of the temporal power, the views of any one are the views of all. They may disagree on all other subjects. On this, they had but one sentiment;—the temporal power was to be maintained and defended at all hazards, and by every means in their power. On this subject, there was no doubt, no hesitancy. This calm conviction and steadiness of purpose marks every act of their administration.

They looked not to the immediate morrow. These dominions were to be transmitted intact, and that power unimpaired, to their successors for the benefit of all future generations. Nothing could be tried to-day, that might have to be cancelled to-morrow. Owing to this cool thoughtfulness, the Papal government can seldom hope for the approval of the impatient present. Men hurrying hotly from one scheme and one device to another, can hardly appreciate the slow but sure progress of the Roman States. They decry, they oppose it accordingly, and their revolutionary efforts have more than once sadly overturned the work of years. But the Popes, true to their mission, have, as often, quietly returned to their task and resumed their work anew.

What! is Rome, that is to-day to all Christendom, what ancient Rome was to the pagan world,—Rome, whose diadem was not lost but changed,—"*commutatum*" as St. Thomas says "*de temporali in spirituale*"—is she now to lose this high prerogative of hers, and relapse again into heathenism. Never. The Eternal City shall not fall into the hands of those who now seek to get possession of her. Neath their unholy rule, a sample of which we have seen in '48, the holy city of St. Peter would become the cess-pool of all that is base and vile in humanity. She would surpass in infamy the Rome of the very worst days of the degenerate and dissolute empire.

Men decry the Roman government and call for the storming of the Capitol. But what guarantee of any better state of things do they offer us, should the Pontifical government disappear? None whatever. And yet Rome is to be kept in a state of continual alarm by these clamorings! It is indeed hard to understand the cold indifference with which the cabinets of Europe behold the most august guardian of all law and order outraged and insulted,— the apathy with which they look on, while the palladium of all authority, human and divine, is daily dragged in the mire and trampled under foot by a vile rabble in the name of progress. The decree of Mazzini that the final blow is to be now dealt to the Papal rule, is received by his fanatical adherents as quite definitive. He it was, be it remembered, who first broached that "modern idea" that the Papacy of itself is sufficiently powerful and efficient for all its ends without the States of the Church. To this day, Mazzini dates all his documents from that blessed era of his, 1848. There was an act passed at Turin a few years ago, declaring Rome the capital of the new kingdom of Italy. We have since had the famous convention of the 15th. of September, and the Italian parliament has been transferred to Florence; but, though repeatedly asked to do so, the Italian government has persistently refused to annul the statute in regard to Rome. It must remain in the statute books as an insult to the Holy Father and a standing menace to his government.

"The language of the diplomatical dispatches, emanating from the Italian ministers, reminds one very forcibly", says the Bishop of Orleans, "of the cloak-covered dagger of the carbonari." The modernized king of modernized Italy, still talks of Rome as his capital. "Italy," he says, "has begun to be, but is not yet complete." *L'Italia è fatta ma non compiuta.*

And but lately, in his reply to the address of the parliament, he assured them that the Roman question should be settled in the manner he and they desire. Side by side with all these open and official declarations, there is the "Roman National Committee" publicly announcing itself as the organ of the Italian government, with the avowed object of working by all manner of means to bring about a revolution against the rule of the sovereign Pontiff. There is besides the "Committee of the Capitol," the "ARRABBIATI" and others, who are at no pains to conceal their impatience, and want at all hazards to hurry on the catastrophe.

Thus on all sides is the Pontifical government menaced and kept in constant alarm, and the more savagely do these bands of robbers and assassins display their hatred to its rule, the more encouragement and sympathy do they meet with from many whom the world is surprised to see in such a connection.

Despite of all his surrounding dangers, the venerable and saintly Pontiff is still to be seen at the Vatican, perfectly fearless, craving no protection from the powers of earth, but reposing his whole trust in heaven, with the most confident assurance of final victory. For his city, Rome, he has but the holy regards of an anxious and affectionate father. Her inhabitants he loves, as indeed he does the whole human race, with a warm, undying love. With charity in his heart, and words of pardon on his lips,

there he stands to-day, to bless even his enemies.
Truly a sublime spectacle this, and one worthy of
Him, whose vicegerent he is upon earth. And for
our part, even should those with whom it rests to
do so, choose Barabbas and shout "Away with
Pius," nevertheless at the sad sight, we must only in
our tears put up the prayer: "Lord, forgive them,
for they know not what they do."

Never since the fall of the Byzantine empire did
the political aspect of Europe look so gloomy as at
the present day. Diplomacy is but the shifts of expediency from hour to hour. No fixed principles
or ideas rule the counsels of statesmen. We have
nothing but "modern ideas," and "modern ideas"
in honest phrase is simply this, that all manner of
means, cunning, deceit, treachery, violence, may be
employed to attain our ends, and that might is one
and the same thing with right. These "modern
ideas" are not after all quite new ones. They were
known, and, alas! too generally acted upon in different parts of Europe during different periods of
the middle ages. But there is this difference between
those times and ours, that as club-law then, was
only maintained by individuals, so it was only individuals who suffered from it; whereas that law in
our days, accepted for the regulation of society, is
driving the human family headlong to destruction.

Right, that once stood on the sacred foundation
of Christian faith and justice, and was exercised in
the name of the eternal truth, and in accordance
with the ethical idea, is now a mere speculation. It is
determined only by the prejudices of the moment,

and right is co-extensive with the word might. A minister of state could have latterly employed the expression, "might precedes right," and acted thereupon, only because such is the idea that rules in modern Europe. European international law is done away with. "Whatever is, is right," said Pope. To-day he might say "whatever can be." The rights of a nation now are limited only by its power. Fear of the more mighty, is the only principle that rules princes and peoples. Relying solely on the strength of their armaments, they are watching each other in feverish anxiety, each striving to outstrip the other in increasing the power and efficiency of its means of warfare. The common plea is, that wars will be thus the sooner ended, whereas in reality, by the termination of a war now-a-days, no finale is arrived at all. War is but a mere local scuffle, in which he comes off best, who is, for the moment, best prepared. At the conclusion, things are as unsettled as before. We are left with the dark prospect of another bloody war looming up in the immediate future. Let us ask is the Crimean war all over? Has Sadowa, or the needle-gun terminated the German war? To neither question can an affirmative answer be given. Nay, we may assert that the solution of any of the great questions that now agitate the European mind, cannot be arrived at by material force. A policy based on such grounds is degrading, is immoral By the very attainment of its end, it would defeat itself; for its success would result in the complete dissolution of European society.

The writer has composed the following pages for those only, whose tastes or occupations will not allow them to enter on a profound study of the subject. Accordingly he has omitted to refer to many documents, that would only weary such readers, and which, for the rest, it would be needless to quote for those well versed in history. These latter must be familiar with the grounds on which he rests his arguments, and no doubt have the documents at hand. For several chapters, the *chefs d'œuvres* of Roman scholars are his guide. A few of these will be cited in the course of the work, as those of GERBET and GREGOROVIUS as well as the works of DR. DOELLINGER.

One word now, in conclusion. In treating the subject of this work, we are conscious that we shall have to deal with questions of vital importance to the Church and to society. Though approaching our task with an honest love of truth, and extremely anxious to be correct in all our statements and conclusions, we are nevertheless fully aware that we are liable to err and to mistake. Wherefore we humbly and respectfully submit the following pages, as well as all else that we may write, to the judgment of that authority, which is alone infallible—to the judgment of the See of Peter.

EINSIEDELN, Feast of St. Peter's See at Rome, 1867.

PART THE FIRST.

Commutatum de temporali in spirituale.
Rome was changed from an earthly into a spiritual Empire.
(*St. Thomas, Expositio in II. Thess.*, C. II, Lect. 4.)

I.
INTRODUCTORY.

THE year 1867 brings us the eighteenth centenary anniversary of the day consecrated to the memory of the great Prince of the Apostles, St. Peter. It was in the year of the christian era 67, that Peter freely shed his blood at Rome in witness of that faith of which his divine Master had constituted him the fast foundation.

Never was dignity so exalted conferred on mortal man, as was conferred on Peter by the Redeemer, never duty so sublime; and faithfully was that high duty performed by the disciple through the aid of Him who enjoined it. Peter, though naturally hasty and enthusiastic, was also timid and changeable. But, in consequence of his election as chief of the Twelve, he acquired by grace the firmness of a rock, and was never more to waver. He now took the place of his divine Master upon earth, as the foundation of that structure erected by Him for the saving of the nations. Peter became, in Christ's own stead, the visible head of the Church. He made Rome the capital of Christ's world-wide spiritual empire. Nero condemned Peter to death, and thought thereby he put an end at once to Peter's career and Peter's work. He little fancied that in putting Peter to the cruel death of the cross upon the Janiculum, he was but furthering the very thing he wished to obstruct—he was but linking Peter and Peter's name forever to that city, which had been chosen to be the capital of the Christian world. The tyrant's purpose was foiled by the very means whereby he sought to effect it, and the designs of God accomplished. Nowhere can we so clearly see how the malice of men is made, in the end, to work out the designs of God, as in the founding of His Church, and His continual guidance thereof. Those who, in their little day, fancied themselves masters of fate, and believed they were shaping the course of history, turn out to have been only instruments in the hands of Providence to bring about its own wise ends.

As the birth of our Divine Redeemer was the all important point of the world's history, so was the coming of Peter to Rome the great turning point in the history of the city of Romulus. Neither event was much known or noticed at the time. Christ was born and the world went on its way. St. Peter preached and died for the faith at Rome, and the city after, seemed just what it was before. The germs from which were to spring such mighty consequences, needed a long time to open, develop and take root in the soil. Their growth was so unmarked at the time, that the keenest observers of human events, Tacitus, for example, and other contemporary writers, either make no mention at all of Christianity, or only speak of it incidentally as a thing of no moment.

Yet Rome and St. Peter are thenceforward inseparably connected, and through Peter, Rome was endowed with immortality. Other cities, as other empires, rose and fell as their mission was fulfilled, or as the circumstances which gave them birth passed away. Rome alone has obtained the high title of the "Eternal City." The foundations of that everlasting kingdom which Christ established, were laid by Peter within her walls, and this it is that makes Rome immortal. On the tree of her earthly glory, was grafted a sapling of a nobler and a higher stock, one destined to produce fruits and flowers of heavenly wisdom and grace, throughout all ages and all time. In Rome, as in no other city, is one reminded at every step, that man may and can live or die for an idea,—for the ideal. Peter is the incarnation of that idea. Take Peter's successor away, and there is no earthly reason why that city on the banks of the Tiber, should not fade away at once into a fishing village. Without the Popes, it had been such long since. And they now talk of depriving the Pope of his sovereignty!—of driving him out of Rome! and even some besotted Romans are not unwilling to participate in the crime. Should the sad event ever come to pass, Rome will find that this patricide will also be her own suicide.

II.
THE CITY AT THE TIME OF ST. PETER'S FIRST VISIT.

THE best authorities that have reached us on the subject of early Christian Rome place St. Peter's first arrival in the capital, in the year 42, or about the early part of the reign of Claudius.

Rome as the capital city of the known world, had then attained the summit of her glory. Under the Republic, the city could boast of only a very few stately buildings. They were simple monuments of Roman worship and Roman story. But when freedom was lost, this sublime simplicity also disappeared. With her inward corruption, commenced the outward glory of Rome. The decline of Roman virtue prepared the Romans for slavery, and the Cæsars found little difficulty in imposing their yoke on a people already debased in morals. Still the pride as well as the pleasures of these masters of the world, had to be gratified. This, the Cæsars did, with treasures brought from the four corners of the globe,— with the rich booty wrested from the stripped and plundered provinces. While he had the circus and the baths, the luxurious Roman gave little thought to liberty. In lieu of the simple monuments of the ancient Republic, he was now given to behold those monuments of splendor and of art, with which the emperors embellished the capital. Augustus found Rome a confused agglomeration of miserable dwellings and ill-laid streets. He could justly boast before his death, that he had given Rome a new appearance,—that he found it a city of brick and mortar, and left it a city of marble.

Each succeeding year witnessed the erection of additional private, as well as public buildings of magnificence. Rome spread into immense proportions. Temples, theatres, baths, gardens, pleasure-grounds, all of the most imposing grandeur, were gradually constructed. Of statutes in pure marble, the number was infinite, and such was the demand at this time for every species of work in stone, that, besides her own two millions of inhabitants, the city supported quite a population of foreign artists, stone-cutters and masons.

The pride of the city was the forum, that stood in the centre, underneath the Capitol. This was overlooked by the ten thousand splendid palaces, villas and gardens, that sloped up the sides of the surrounding hills. This forum, once the people's own house and home, had now lost under the Cæsars its peculiar political significance. In compensation for this loss, it was richly adorned all round with the costliest works of art, and was made in a manner the chief repository of ancient traditions. Side by side, however, with this grand memento of other days, the emperors were careful to erect still richer and more costly forums, as monuments of the imperial power and glory. These, with their immense yet beautiful architectural proportions, finished too in every detail with the most artistic skill, were unquestionably the finest monuments of the city of the Cæsars. Through sixteen large gates, the Romans had egress to the surrounding country, and no less than eight hundred and twenty paved high-roads led into the different provinces, forming with their intersections, a network of easy thoroughfares, beginning at the golden milestone erected by Augustus in the forum at the foot of the Capitol, as the central point of the empire, and spreading thence over the known world.

Such was Rome, when St. Peter in the beginning of the reign of Claudius, first stood within her gates. What impression the imperial city then made upon the poor fisherman, brought up in a little inland town of Palestine, we can only gather from his designating her a "Babylon," a word whereby the Jews were wont to signify the lowest depths of immorality and corruption.

III.
ST. PETER'S ARRIVAL IN ROME.

ONE of the early Fathers describes, in a clear and naive manner, the supernatural character of St. Peter's mission and the task he undertook in consequence.

Picture to yourself an unknown, unlettered stranger, entering one afternoon that capital of wealth and luxury. He is clad in humble garb, and his neglected hair and bushy beard bespeak his utter indifference to fashion. The heavy dust on his long mantle, as well as the worn-out sandals on his otherwise bare feet, argue of long and weary travelling. He halts for a moment with his few companions at the Porto Navali, and inquires his way to the Jewish quarter of the city beyond the Tiber. He likewise informs himself of the names of the principal monuments that strike his eye in the distance. From the stone on which he sits to rest, he can descry the lofty summits of the Capitol and the temple of Jupiter. While sitting by that gate, and meditating on the scene before him, one of the numberless stone-cutters that were then at Rome, steps up, and, asking after news and this and that, enters into a conversation with the stranger. The following dialogue between him and Peter took place:—

Pagan—"Stranger, may I ask what brings you to Rome? Perhaps, I can be of service to you."

Peter—"I have come to make the Unknown God known, and to have Him worshipped instead of idols."

Pagan—"What do you mean? Hercules! this is something to chat about with my friends this evening as we stroll 'round the Forum. If you've no objection I'd like to hear a little more on this subject. But say, first, from what country are you?"

Peter—"I belong to a people that the Romans hate and despise, and whom they have more than once driven from their city. We are now, however, allowed to live here. My countrymen dwell, as I am told, not far from here. Yonder is their quarter beyond the Tiber;—I am from Judea."

Pagan—"You are, no doubt, some person of note among your own people? You hold some high position in your country,—eh?"

Peter—"Do you see those fishermen at the river?—that's my trade. I have spent most of my life in fishing, making and mending my nets. Riches, or lands I have none."

Pagan—"You must have studied philosophy, then, after quitting your trade, and learned eloquence in the schools of the Rhetoricians to rely on for a living."

Peter—"I am but a poor unlettered man."

Pagan—"But, then, I can't see how you intend to make a living! However, I dare say the worship of this great god you speak of will so take, that you'll need no other recommendation to be able to get along."

Peter—"I rather think you are mistaken. This God Whom I announce, was Himself put to death and crucified with two highwaymen."

Pagan—"Well, then, and what have you to tell us about such a queer god?"

Peter—"I have to preach a doctrine which will seem folly to the proud and licentious, and which will condemn those vices to which your city has erected temples."

Pagan—"And you are going to preach this here in Rome!"

Peter—"Certainly, and not only here in Rome, but the whole world over."

Pagan—"And for how long?"

Peter—"Forever."

Pagan—"By Jove! a pretty heavy undertaking, this; and let me tell you, unless you're backed by able friends, I rather fear the beginning will be the end. But I suppose you have some of the Cæsars, or wealthy patricians, or the philosophers already on your side?"

Peter—"Nay, sir, nothing of the kind. On the contrary, I must bid the rich renounce their wealth, and call on the philosophers to bow their necks to the yoke of faith; and to Cæsar, must I say, that he is henceforth neither god nor high-priest."

Pagan—"Tush, man, tush!—Don't you see, at once, that such language, instead of arraying them on your side, would set them all against you and against your schools, should you start any?—What could you do then?"

Peter—"Die."

Pagan—"Indeed, I can't help remarking this last is the most likely thing you said yet. Well, I must be going. I feel obliged for your entertaining conversation, and hope we'll meet again—good-by!—The poor crazy fool! And yet, 'tis a pity, for he seems to be a fine fellow." —

This dialogue, though of course imaginary, depicts pretty fairly the real state of affairs, as well as the tone of the popular mind at the time of St. Peter's arrival in Rome. It was indeed very natural that his undertaking should seem sheer folly to a Roman citizen. Paganism was fast rooted in the minds of men,—in their passions, prejudices and ideas. Idolatry was close entwined with the empire, and whoever should attempt to tear it down, would become thereby, the open enemy of the state, and the governing and the governed alike would adjudge such a one guilty of high treason. Even those who in their hearts derided and despised the state-worship, looked upon it, nevertheless, as a useful, if not a necessary means of carrying on the government.

But in God's decree it was written of Rome:— "Peter shall succeed Romulus and the Cæsars."

IV.

THE APOSTLE'S PREACHING.

All St. Peter's discourses to the Romans show who fully impressed he was with the importance and significance of the place. God's kingdom was transferred from Jerusalem to Rome. The germ of divine faith which had for centuries remained undeveloped in the soil of Palestine and quite unknown to the rest of mankind, was now transplanted to the world's capital, where it was destined to grow up into a mighty tree overshadowing all the nations of the earth. What Peter primarily insists on at Rome, is the universality of the kingdom of God. In the cross, is salvation for all,—all, without exception,—and all stand equally in need of this salvation.

The personality of Jesus,—"Jesus forever praiseworthy"—is prominently brought forward. All Christians form one kingdom of which Christ is king, Whom all must obey and serve. On earth too, one alone ruled, who was both lord and god, (*Dominus et Deus,*) whether it was a Tiberius, a Claudius, a Nero or a Domitian, names, than which, none more infamous were ever written on the page of history. St. Peter's preaching now all turns upon the life and works of Jesus, from the commencement of his public ministry to the Resurrection. He shows how, when the fulness of time was come, those various prophecies relating to the Messiah,—prophecies not wholly unknown to the Romans,—were all fulfilled in the person of Christ. He dwells on the poverty and lowliness in which the Redeemer was pleased to appear in this world, to the end he might elevate mankind above the paltry, fleeting things of earth. He holds up to their admiration, the heavenly wisdom of His doctrine, and details the miracles he wrought, the prophecies he uttered, and the circumstances of his Passion, Death and Resurrection. All this, St. Peter's devoted disciple, Mark, penned in that Gospel, which he composed under his master's own eyes. It was at the request of some of the Roman Christians "*a quibusdam Cæsarianis equitibus,*" that Peter had his disciple to draw up these few, short, simple, but vivid sketches. He exhorts those whom he has won to the faith in Rome, to be such as he says they are, when writing to the Christians of Asia Minor:—that, as through the grace of Christ they were made heirs of the Promise, so should they study to be perfect after the fashion of their divine Model, bearing in themselves the likeness of Christ, not like Him indeed, as partaking in the divine nature, but like Him in virtue and in holiness. He tells them, that by their faith, they must acquire humility; through humility, knowledge; through knowledge, forbearance; through forbearance, patience; through patience, godliness; through godliness, brotherly-love and through this, charity, which is the fulfilment of the whole law and the bond of perfection.

Such the doctrine which the Prince of the Apostles preached to the astonished Romans, who already knew little or much of all the religions of the Eastern as well as the Western nations, but had now no religion of their own. Their ablest moralists with all their philosophy, such as Seneca, Pliny and Tacitus, had never dreamt of doctrine so sublime; nor had the Pantheon which admitted within its gates all the religions of the earth, anything that could bear comparison with this. And yet, with God's grace, the moral and spiritual regeneration of the city was already being effected under the philosophers' very eyes, through this sublime teaching.

V.

THE EARLY CHRISTIANS OF ROME.

DOUBTLESS St. Peter's first little congregation at Rome was composed of those Jews, who had gone for the yearly celebration to Jerusalem, and had been converted by the Apostle's first sermons after the descent of the Holy Ghost. They dwelt in Rome with those of their own nation, who exclusively inhabited a small district of the city near the Porta Capena, beyond the Tiber. By the zeal of this little Jew-Christian congregation, the knowledge of the Gospel was soon spread among the Romans proper, and no doubt, in the higher circles of society, too. To this Jew-quarter, all the merchants of the world thronged to sell and purchase wares. It is not unlikely that Peter's first lodgings in Rome were situated on the great aristocratic street, called "*Vicus Corneliorum.*" On this street, was the palace, or mansion of that noble Cornelius, who, by divine admonition was baptised together with his whole family by Peter at Cæsarea. In this wise, we can account for the fact of so many noble names appearing among the earliest Roman Christians. St. Peter was soon introduced by the Centurion to the head of the Cornelian family, the senator Cornelius Pudens. This nobleman's house, situated on the Viminal hill, was the first Christian Church in the city. The senator's whole family, his mother Priscilla, his daughters Pudentiana and Praxes, and his sons or grandsons Timothy and Novatus, all became saints of the Church. Pudens himself died a martyr, and was the father of a family of martyrs. Priscilla devoted herself to the work of burying those who died for Christ in that catacomb now called by her name, and which was probably a private family vault. St. Pudentiana was so active in spreading the truths of the Christian religion, that she at one time brought no less than six hundred and ninety persons to the pope, all so well instructed and prepared by herself, that he had nothing to do, but baptise them. These two sisters Praxes and Pudentiana, with the most heroic self-sacrifice and at constant peril of their lives, interred the bodies of upwards of three thousand martyrs.

The consul Flavius Clemens, who was the nearest of kin to the emperor Domitian, together with his wife, Flavia Domitilla, and his niece of the same name, and still greater renown, as well as his two sons, who had been raised to the dignity of Cæsars, all ably co-operated in these good works with the family of Cornelius. The sons, Vespasian and Domitian, were adopted by the tyrant Domitian, who entrusted their education to Quintilian. Their father was condemned to death in the year ninety-six, their mother banished to the isle Pandataria:— the niece, Flavia Domitilla, who was also niece of the emperor Titus, was baptised by St. Peter, and soon converted her mother Plantilla, two officers of her household, and many others, who were all baptised by the Apostle. Flavia Domitilla made use of her vast resources to support the poor and relieve the wretched. The better to acquire Christian humility, she laid aside all rank and state, and was a living proof of the effectiveness of St. Peter's preaching. She devoted herself particularly to the care of those slaves, who, becoming useless to their masters by reason of old age or sickness, were cast helpless on the world. These, she housed and fed, and, together with her two assistants, Nereus and Achilleus, provided for their every want. The hospital or house in which these were kept, was at the same time a church. The site it occupied is that on which now stands the basilica of St. Clement.

A church springing up as that of Rome did, can, of course, have little documents of its early history; save the acts of its martyrs. From these, we learn that the infant church already numbered among her members individuals from every rank and grade of society, patricians and plebeians, rich and poor, masters and slaves. The number of the poor who almost immediately accepted the faith, was immense, and of the higher classes, besides the names already mentioned, several others have come down to us of the noblest families of Rome. The perusal of these acts is most interesting and useful. Not a shade of human joy or sorrow crosses the human heart, that has not been expressed in those ancient archives of the Roman church. Of the "adorable Jesus," they speak with all the fire and fervency of early love, which makes St. Jerome somewhere say, that "the hearts of the faithful were still warmed by the hot blood of Jesus." Hence could St. Paul who had come to Rome about the year sixty-two, when writing to the Philippians, send them greeting "from the saints at Rome, especially from those of the imperial household."

We see here, how edified the Apostle of the gentiles was with this flourishing young church in which the faith had already taken such fast root. The Christians at Rome, hearing of his arrival at Pateoli, went out in great numbers many miles on the road to meet him, to express their love, and the joy his coming gave them. Seeing at a glance the piety of these Christians, the Apostle's heart was gladdened, and he fervently thanked God for the sight he saw. No doubt, this great joy of the Apostle, at witnessing the fervent piety of the Romans, was motived by his knowledge of the important role which that church was to play in the Christian world. These were indeed days of wonderful virtue, and, in those glorious beginnings of the primitive Church, may be discovered the great development she was afterwards to attain. For the first few years, the spread of the Gospel was quick, silent, unobstructed. The Roman church had not yet been hunted into the catacombs. But, in the petty annoyances whereby the Roman magistrates already begin to harrass the Apostles and several of their disciples, we can clearly discern the coming storm. It soon burst over that devoted church, and raged with all the fury of earth and hell upon her, for more than three centuries. It was the war of fallen human nature against that high morality of the Christian religion which was now forcing itself on the human race.

VI.
THE CHAIR OF ST. PETER.

In the neighborhood of Trajan's forum, the most magnificent of all the imperial forums or courts—on that spot, where now, on the loftiest column of ancient Rome stands a life-size statue of St. Peter, was in early days the dwelling of senator Pudens. The Prince of the Apostles who was enjoying this senator's hospitality, used to assemble the faithful in that house for instructions, and for the celebration of the divine mysteries. The history of a few monuments of Christian Rome, is bound up with this house of Pudens. Of one only, shall we now speak.

The senator's chair of state, the curule chair on which he sate when transacting public business, St. Peter used to occupy in delivering these homilies to the faithful. Hence comes it that the pope and all the bishops are wont to sit, as a sign of dignity, while they address the people. This very same chair,—the Cathedra,—that Peter then made use of, is now St. Peter's Chair,—the Apostolic Chair, the Holy See, or Seat. From such chairs of state—Cathedræ—have the bishops' churches derived the name of cathedrals. But the Pope's church called after the very identical chair that Peter occupied, is designated, in token of its being the highest authority in the world, the Chair or See of Peter, the Papal Chair, or the Holy See.

This chair is of wood, with ornamental arches of exquisite workmanship, supported by pillars of pure gold. Round the back are mythological figures in ivory, carved in bass-relief. The workmanship belongs to the very best period of ancient Roman art. The deeds of Heraclius are represented in the bass-relief. This proves clearly that the chair was originally destined for heathen use, as it is by no means likely that one made for a Christian bishop would be thus ornamented. Besides it can hardly be admitted that such a degree of perfection in the art of sculpture was attained at a later epoch. There are iron rings attached to the chair, through which rods used to be passed, when it was taken from one place to another. Such portable chairs began to be used by the Roman nobles in the reign of Claudius. Regarding this novelty, Justus Lipsius remarks: "At the time of Augustus there were none of these portable chairs—the litter was alone in fashion. After Claudius the litter was seldom seen; the chair took its place." It is quite likely then, that the senator Pudens, one of the wealthiest of the Roman patricians, who could leave his daughter the boundless wealth he did, was among the first to follow the rising fashion, and got this very costly piece of furniture made, while St. Peter was still his guest.

It would appear as if this wooden chair partook in a manner of the unchangeableness of the Holy See, of which it is the material representative.

This monument of the infant Church is already upwards of eighteen hundred years old, and has passed uninjured through all the troubles and revolutions that have in that time fallen upon Rome and the Holy See. Some two centuries ago, it was encased in bronze, and now stands in the tribune or choir of St. Peter's. The chair or case in bronze is supported by four figures representing four of the greatest doctors of the Church—two Greek, Athanasius and Chrysostomus, and two Latin, Ambrose and Augustine. In the midst is an altar dedicated to the Virgin and all the canonized popes. It is called the altar of the Chair of Peter, and was lately repaired and consecrated anew by Pius the Ninth, the two hundred and sixtieth successor of St. Peter.

VII.

THE PERSECUTION UNDER NERO—ST. PETER'S MARTYRDOM.

A SHORT time after founding the Church in Rome, St. Peter left the city, giving charge of the congregation in his absence to Linus and Cletus. He did not return till the year 64. Nero was then emperor, and during his reign it was, that the first storm of persecution burst over the Roman church.

Hatred of Christianity was at first only indirectly the cause of this persecution. It was only when the tyrant's thirst for blood was well aroused, that hate of the Christian name began to be the one simple motive of this fearful persecution. Nero conceived the silly wish to build the world's capital anew and call it after his own name, Neropolis. To this wish is ascribed by cotemporary writers the dreadful conflagration that broke out in Rome during Nero's reign. It completely destroyed three out of the fourteen quarters of the city, and left seven others little better than a pile of blackened ruins. The fire raged six days and seven nights.

Notwithstanding the city was restored at a most lavishing expense and in an incredibly short space of time, the Romans could not altogether forgive Nero, though now prodigal in his liberality to the sufferers, the crime of causing the fire. He now lost the attachment even of these degenerate Romans, who had so long basely clung to him.

To remove the odium and the consequences of this crime from himself, the emperor laid it to the charge of the Christians. These, he knew, were already out of favor with the Romans. Wretches were bribed to accuse them publicly, and thousands — *"ingens multitudo"* — must die for a crime they had never thought of. Tacitus informs us that their penalties were invariably accompanied with wanton indignities. Some were cast to wild beasts, torn by dogs, or fastened to the cross; while others were smeared over with pitch, hung up and set fire to, to light the streets by night. In this manner Nero had his Vatican gardens lit up, the very ground on which now stands the Vatican Palace and St. Peter's Church, the Capitol of Christendom.

This persecution was the baptism of blood of the infant Roman church. It lasted till the tyrant's death in the year 69.

After his return to Rome in the year 64, Peter addressed his epistles to the churches of Asia Minor. In these we discover forebodings of the coming persecution. It is his part, as a good shepherd, to watch over those committed to his keeping in all troubles and dangers. St. Paul was also now returned to Rome. Though chained to one of his keepers, he fearlessly continued to preach the Gospel, so that his prison in the Via Lata was made to serve as a church.

In view of his approaching death, the Prince of the Apostles was careful to provide a successor for the high office of Chief Bishop. Accordingly, in addition to these already consecrated, he elevated Clement, his own disciple, to the episcopal dignity. Peter's wife had followed him to Rome during the persecution, and there preceded him to martyrdom. Eusebius, on the authority of St. Clement, tells us that as she was led forth by the executioners, Peter went to meet her. The joyful alacrity with which she faced her doom, made a deep impression on the Apostle. He earnestly thanked God for the happy lot that had been assigned her, who had been the companion of his life. He called to her by name, and simply said: "Think of the Lord." The memory of the happy death she died, was not without its effect upon himself, when he was soon after led forth to meet the same fate.

At this time Peter did not think the day of his own death so nigh. There stands on the Appian way, at a short distance from the city, a little chapel or oratory which is the object of a pious and affecting tradition concerning St. Peter. It appears that the Apostle, following the counsel of his divine Master, "When they persecute you in one city, flee into another," was about to make his escape from Rome at this time. He was forced to this step by the importunities of the faithful who begged him for their sakes to provide for his own safety. On the night of his intended flight, as he was starting from the house that occupied the site where now the chapel stands, he was met by Christ, going with his cross towards the city. Peter in astonishment asked Him: "Lord whither?"—Christ answered: "I come here to Rome to get crucified again." Peter understood His meaning: he returned to the city and remained directing his flock till seized by the satellites of Nero.

In the year 67, the emperor returned from his literary (!) travels in Greece. 'Mid the scenes of cruelty which Suetonius describes, Nero's thirst for blood was kindled anew. At one time he thought of putting the whole senate to death, because he fancied they were not quite as docile as was proper. In another whim he resolved to extirpate Christianity. Peter was arrested and confined in the Mamertine prison near the Capitol. During his confinement he went on with the work of conversion, as Paul, who was now likewise in the Mamertine, had done in the Via Lata. The jailors, with forty-seven others, were in this way gained to Christ. After nine months imprisonment he was led forth to execution. Those condemned to the cross were not put to death at the same place with those who were to die by the sword. Paul was among the latter, and obtained his crown on the road to Ostia, while Peter was taken to the place of crucifixion either on the Janiculum or on the Vatican hill. Tradition is divided as to which of these two spots it was, on which he suffered. For the rest, both are very near each other.

An inscription placed between two small pillars on the Ostian road, indicates the place where the two Apostles took their last farewell of each other on earth. According to this, the Apostle of the gentiles first addresses Peter: "Peace be with thee, thou, the foundation of the church, the pastor of all Christ's flock." Whereupon St. Peter replies: "Go in peace, thou, the teacher of all that is good, thou, the leader of the righteous on the path of salvation." Though it is very probable these salutes were never in reality exchanged, yet they express what must naturally have passed through the minds of both these heroes of the faith at that moment. The two had done more for Rome and the world than was ever fabled of Romulus and Remus.

Peter is now on his way to the place of execution. The prophecy of his divine Master that "in his old age his hands should be streched out and bound, and he should be led by another whither he would not," is about to be fulfilled. The mystery of that "Follow me, thou," is revealed. Peter was a true unflinching follower of Christ in his life, he is to be such now in his death. He was nailed to the cross, and according to the most reliable traditions was, at his own request, crucified with his head downwards. The generally received authorities say his death took place in the year 67.

As to the fact of St. Peter's crucifixion at Rome there never was a serious doubt. The entire history of the early church bears witness to it. The doubts which infidel writers from time to time thought to raise on the subject, could not for a moment withstand the strong tide of historical and traditional evidence testifying to the event, and dating as far back as the first century. Even before the close of this century, St. Peter's martyrdom was a fact so universally known that St. John could content himself with a bare allusion thereto, to be generally understood.

VIII.

PETER THE VISIBLE HEAD OF THE VISIBLE CHURCH.

The great boon Christ procured us in the Redemption is, that we may all be one in God, and one with God, and He left us His own merits as the means whereby to attain this holy unity.

The night before He suffered, after giving the Twelve His sacred body and blood, both to signify and to cause this unity between Him and His, He prayed to His heavenly Father and said:—"And not for them only do I pray, but for those also who through their word shall believe in Me: that they all may be one as Thou, Father, in Me, and I in Thee, that they also may be one in Us; that the world may believe that Thou hast sent Me."

Now this one life, originating in the Redeemer, should quicken all mankind—it should be, as it were, the heart's-blood of the race, and so would there be one faith, one baptism, one Lord, and one God. To this end, did Christ found His Church; this, the meaning of her existence; this, her place in the world's history, and, therefore, must she last through all time. This unity of the faithful, in Christ and with Christ, must be visible, must present itself to the senses, that mankind may be able to learn the high mission of the Saviour.

Had Christ chosen to abide with us in a visible manner He could Himself be our visible head. He would govern and arrange all things, and be the centre of unity, from which all that is Christian should radiate. But as He did not think fit to remain forever with us in the flesh, save under the mysterious sacramental veils, He had needs leave us some vice-gerent who should act in His name, and be for us a visible bond of that union which the Redemption procured us, the visible head of all the faithful. After the three-fold protestation of his faith and love, Peter was chosen by his divine Master to be this visible head.

What now, let us imagine, must be the anxiety of a frail mortal man, placed thus at the head of a church, whose members are scattered the world over, and who has to contend, all at once, against those who hate and war against the Christian name, against the ambition and avarice of princes, against infidelity, heresy and the vicissitudes and revolutions of society? Christ led St. Peter, as it were, by the hand to Rome. But this did not seem to smoothen, but rather to increase the difficulty. For by the very fact that Rome was the centre of earthly power, it only seemed the more difficult ever to make it the centre of Christianity, the see of Christ's vicar upon earth. And yet, Peter is to-day in Rome, wearing the triple crown, and, for the last eighteen hundred years, has borne unshaken the burden of his high office. Kingdoms, he saw rise around him that are now no more, while ambassadors from the nations of the earth are at his court, and he sends his own

—*a latere*—to the different potentates of Christendom, and his servants to the farthest ends of the earth, even to those nations, and tribes, and peoples, that are yet unknown to history. He rules at Rome, and is the only ruler on earth that can say, he neither built, nor conquered, nor bought, nor was given, his city, and yet that he is that city's very inmost life, that he quickens and vivifies it as the blood does the human body.

Here is in truth a strange thing in history. This unusual, and, historically, almost inexplicable elevation of Christ's Vicar, the successor of St. Peter, has its real foundation in the eternal decrees of God Who governs this world by His Providence, Who raises up the mighty and dashes them again as He lists to the dust, and Who appoints years and limits to the nations. Though disposing all things according to His divine Will, His action on human events is hidden from our ken. Our purpose here, is to trace in regard to the Holy See, the mysterious workings of God as far as history lifts the veil and unfolds them to our view.

The unity of all the members under their one head, is the best witness to the succession of our church from the Apostles, a proof, so to say, of our authenticity. Without visible union of some sort, there can be neither spiritual nor intellectual union of any kind among men. The idea of an invisible communion between individuals scattered the world over who never saw each other, is sheer nonsense. St. Paul knew nothing of such a union or communion. When speaking of individuals, he says that each and every one must be a part of the one whole, that the same spirit must pervade the different members, and that each with this one self-same spirit must be animated. In another place he inculcates the necessity of this unity, employing the simile drawn from the different parts of the human body, each part having its own respective functions to perform, yet all making up one body subject to one head. The Apostle's heart seems to beat quicker with joy, as he witnesses with his own eyes what that church is, to which, as to their head, all other churches are to be united in one body. All alike and together gain access to God, Who has united them under one visible head, in one body, and one spirit. It is thus the Apostle of the gentiles conceives and portrays the Church of Christ. It is one body and one soul with its one visible head, Peter. The theory of the church having but spiritual unity is merely the old error of the Docetians, who, already in the days of St. John, the Apostle, fell into heresy regarding Christ's body, maintaining that by this was meant the Christian revelation, Christ's greatest work. This same error, that would formerly make Jesus a mere phantom, would now make Jesus' church an ideal nothing, a mere abstract idea. The thing is so absurd, it is not worth dwelling on.

IX.
THE TRUE CHURCH OF CHRIST IS ROMAN AND CATHOLIC.

It is only through Peter that the Church is the Church, that is, a visible body under one visible head.

From the fact that Peter fixed his see in Rome, that see became the chief Apostolic, the primatial see of Christianity. As Peter's successors can never fail, but must appear to the end of time as bishops of Rome, so is Rome thereby become, in truth, the "Eternal City." Pope after Pope must succeed unto the consummation of the world, and Rome must ever remain, to be the root of that vast tree whose branches stretch from pole to pole. It is only through Rome that the other churches are united with each other. They are one with Rome and so, one with each other. Hence a characteristic mark of all true Christian churches is to be Roman.

As the church, according to Christ's command, is to teach all nations, and as she is, according to the divine promise, to last till the end of time, she is thus Catholic or universal both as to place and time. This twofold Catholicity is one of her essential attributes, and this characteristic of the Church strikes one in a particular manner at Rome.

During the Pontificate of St. Evaristus who in the year 95 followed his predecessors to martyrdom, the Church began to be called Catholic. This name was given her to distinguish those of the true faith from the heretical sects that were already cropping up, especially the Gnostics. Many of these came out of Asia to Rome, and, though cast out from the bosom of the Church for their errors in faith and morals, persisted while a disgrace to the name in calling themselves Christians. We know the salutary severity with which St. Paul treated such unworthy members of the Church. We know also what a horror St. John had of the heretic Cerinth who perverted the doctrine of his divine Master. The Catholic Church in this, as in all else, follows the word and example of the Apostles. Every Catholic knows her jealous laws in regard to heresy, and he is proud to think of the unity and communion of all the faithful which is the result. True he is deprived of the exercise of private judgment in certain matters. But this is merely depriving him of the liberty to err. Such a privation is a boon, not a disadvantage. It is the safeguard whereby the perfect unity and communion of the faithful is preserved. The Church, established for the salvation of men, is Catholic above all else in her charity. Her love, like that of her divine Founder, embraces all mankind from Adam down through all time, past, present, and to come. This charity is kept ever burning by the remembrance of that prayer of her great High-Priest. "Not for these only do I pray, but also for all those who through their word shall believe in Me."

It is very remarkable, that, from the first, a certain analogy was unmistakably claimed by the new Christian Rome with the ancient capital of the world. There was this difference, however, that the one was by a divine ordinance, whereas the other fell out according to the natural course of things. This difference is indeed as wide as the poles are asunder. It should never be overlooked. But, bearing this in mind, we cannot but be struck with the otherwise close analogy drawn from the earliest times by Christian writers between ancient Rome, with her naturally acquired gifts and position in the world, and Christian Rome in what she was made by the divine favor. This is pointedly set forth by St. Clement in his first epistle to the Corinthians. In that church a schism, subsequent to the one spoken of by St. Paul, broke out in Clement's time. The Corinthians sent a deputation to the Pope claiming his advice and assistance to put down the scandal. They complained that some ambitious individuals had formed round themselves a party and sought forcibly to eject certain worthy priests from the churches over which they had been set by the Apostles themselves, in order to get their places. Contrary to all law and precedent, these men undertook to disturb the ecclesiastical affairs of Corinth. They assumed the discharge of pastoral duties as if they had been regularly appointed, and, while they boasted of the righteousness of their lives, they were bringing by their sinful ambition the sorest scandal and anarchy upon the church of Corinth. It was under such circumstances, St. Clement wrote the epistle we have mentioned. It betrays throughout the utmost caution, prudence and forbearance, with rare wisdom and Apostolic earnestness. The vigor of the old republican heroes that made Rome mistress of the world is also clearly discernible in the style of Clement, but the severity and stubborn obstinacy of the old Roman is now softened by the mild spirit of Christianity. Instead of the crooked policy of mere earthly ambition, we find the compassionate love of one who sorrows for the sins of all mankind.

This remarkable epistle is a model of the Christian pastoral, and is, in every respect, worthy of a disciple and successor of St. Peter. Among other things Clement asserts the divine origin of the Christian hierarchy. He shows how the Apostles under the guidance of Christ appointed bishops, priests and deacons over the different churches. They appointed such to succeed themselves in carrying on the work of the Gospel, and, according as some died, others were set up in their stead. They thus established the law of the Apostolic succession. Clement wrote this epistle to the Corinthians in classical Greek about the year 95.

The vigorous, all conquering spirit of ancient Rome is born anew to Christian Rome, and clearly displays itself already, though in a different manner and to a different end.

X.

ST. PETER IN SUBTERRANEAN ROME.

THE catacombs of Rome are the best archives wherein to search for the early history of Christianity. Most of the missing links in that history have been already found in these vaults, and, day after day, others are being exhumed. Scarce a doctrine of the Church or a custom, that is not found expressed, by word or symbol, on the walls, the slabs, or the instruments of worship discovered in the catacombs. Now, if any one idea might be said to predominate in the silent language of these vaults of the dead, it is that of the primacy of St. Peter.

When the persecution under Nero broke out, the Christians of Rome could no longer hold their assemblies in the city. For secresy's sake they betook themselves to these subterranean caverns. The sacred mysteries were celebrated at the crossing of the ways, or in the little excavated chambers of the place. Here too they buried their dead, and here with pious veneration they laid the mangled remains of their numberless martyrs. Two hundred and fifty years had the Christians of Rome to hide themselves thus away in the bowels of the earth. Then, at length, in virtue of their heroic patience and strong endurance, in virtue of the torrents of blood freely shed by their martyrs, were the persecutors overcome. By this baptism of blood was the Church of Rome purified. Subterranean Rome came forth and took possession of the Seven Hills. Peter is lord of the Vatican, and the successor of the Cæsars, Constantine, goes to build him a city on the Bosphorus. Thus did persevering endurance come off triumphant in the end, or as the poet expressed it:—

> "The enduring, not the mighty,
> Win the day and wear the laurels."

To the internal causes that had long been bringing on the dissolution of the Western empire, was now added that terrible invasion of the Northern barbarians, that finds no parallel in the history of the human race. Countless and countless hordes poured down in hot succession from the bleak and barren North upon the fertile fields of Southern Europe. Ere Italy could recover from the devastation and desolation of one flood of barbarism, another and another rolled over her. This continued for generations, and in the confusion into which society was thrown all memory of subterranean Rome, save a few of the most remarkable spots, was completely lost. After a lapse of centuries, this city of the early Christians was discovered, and, by degrees, opened up and explored as Pompeii and Herculaneum. The researches made through its miles and miles of streets, have shed light on many of the misty points of the early history of the Church, and afford the most unmistakable evidence, that the Church of to-day is one in faith and dogma with the Church of the first century.

We can here only cast a glance at one part of this subterranean Rome, that near the Vatican. The neighborhood of the Vatican where Nero had his gardens and circus, came, as Tacitus informs us, to be thought unhealthy, so that people were unwilling to build there. The place was therefore very probably a lonesome one. Here the Christians first began to sink their subterranean dwellings. The remains of the martyrs who suffered in the circus and in those gardens, were here interred together. Here also, but by itself, and with a special monument, was laid the venerated body of St. Peter. The following simple but touching inscription was inscribed on St. Peter's tomb:—"Anacletus, a priest ordained by St. Peter, erected this stone to his memory, and made other tombs for the bishops; he himself is buried here beside the body of St. Peter." Thus did Christianity first take possession of the Vatican. During the persecution, this little grotto of the Vatican was at once the tomb, the oratory, and the see of the Popes. Hither was the curule chair of Pudens transported. St. Peter's successors continued to use this chair both through reverence for the Apostle and as a symbol of that authority, which they inherited from him. There can be no doubt that we owe the preservation of this costly relic to the symbolical meaning which immediately attached to it. This small grotto now contained the germ of that second Rome which Christianity afterwards built up and magnified.

In all these catacombs, especially in that of the Vatican, St. Peter, both in inscriptions and symbols,

invariably occupies a prominent place. From the
first century on, we find a certain figure in many of
these representations that must evidently have been
intended for St. Peter. When the Apostles are represented standing round the Saviour, Peter has a
chair of honor by His side, or is distinguished by
some mark of dignity from the others, to indicate
his pre-eminence. Many of the frescoes represent
Christ holding in his hand a staff or sceptre, the
emblem of authority and regal power, and handing
this sceptre to Peter. In another Peter is represented striking water from a rock with this sceptre, as
did Moses, the leader of God's people of old. One
of these frescoes bears the simple inscription "Petrus," showing he was the personage the artist intended primarily to represent. In another, Christ
appears sitting on a hill and reaching Peter a parchment roll on which is written "The lord gives the
law." Peter, with hands muffled in the folds of his
garment, reverently receives the roll. In another
representation, he is represented as receiving the
keys in like manner. In that age the vice-gerents
of the emperors in the different provinces were thus
invested with the emblems of their office. The
Christian artists wished to indicate that Peter was
made Christ's vicar or vice-gerent upon earth for the
government of His church. In another place, Christ
leaves to Peter His mantle, as Elias formerly left his
to his disciple. This is to signify that the spirit of
the Saviour descended on Peter,—that Peter is the
legitimate successor and heir to His power. Again,
a boat with swelling sails is represented with Paul

a-midships and Peter holding the tiller: at the masthead flies a flag bearing the oft-found motto "The master makes the law."

Numberless are the inscriptions, symbols and figures, in which Peter's supremacy is thus clearly indicated. Never throughout the dark and weary days of that trying persecution was this point lost sight of. And if the upper city still remained the centre and capital of the ancient world, the many and far stretching roads that led to it, served to bring Christians of all nations from the farthest points of the empire to the new Rome below, which was already the centre and capital of Christianity. Among the twelve thousand inscriptions which have been found in the catacombs, we find the names of Christians from Gaul, Spain, Africa, Egypt, Syria, Greece, and different parts of Asia, so that the catacombs prove at once and give us a beautiful illustration of the unity and Catholicity of the Church and of the precedence of the "Eternal City."

XI.

THE CHRISTIAN REGENERATION OF THE CITY,—THE PARADOX OF HISTORY.

WHILE the seed of Christianity was yet hidden in the soil, and was barely noticeable at Rome by the number of the martyrs, the city continued to sink deeper and deeper into vice. Rome became the great sink of heathen iniquity. The moral filth of the world streamed from all directions to the city of the Cæsars. That golden edifice on the Palatine, the imperial palace so luxuriously fitted up and embellished with all that the world could afford, held forth to view without fear or shame the grossest and most abominable crimes.

It was on such ruins, in such a fearfully desolated land, St. Peter fixed his see, that see which was to be the prop of Christendom. It is still the task of Christianity to try its strength against evil, and in the midst of sin and heresy, sin and heresy to combat. This heathen Rome, which the Apostle calls "Babylon," that is, in the language of Judea, the most corrupted of cities, is to be transformed into virtuous Christian Rome.

Here more than anywhere else, did error hold that sway over men's minds which is the right of truth alone. Men, naturally forced to accept that form of worship in which they were brought up as an expression and representation of truth, needed extraordinary proofs and arguments to be able to change their whole system of ideas. How was a Roman of that day to conceive that besides Cæsar whom they named god and lord, another ruled at Rome calling himself "Servant of the Servants of God,"—that, in the prime of life, men should be born again and celebrate with joy their own nativity? When coming to Rome, Peter brought the new spiritual leaven in the folds of his mantle. He told of the Redemption and of the spiritual freedom of all, be they slaves or masters. This it was, with the grace of God, that infused the new soul into mankind. To this end did Christ communicate to His Apostles and disciples the virtue of miracles which, above all others, was conspicuous in St. Peter. Without some supernatural intervention, it were impossible for pagan Rome to be transformed into a Christian city. To effect this transformation, the Apostles and their successors proved their divine mission by miracles. Indeed, the greatest miracle of all was the never failing hecatombs of martyrs, the sight of which, from generation to generation, forced Christianity upon the notice of the wondering Romans. On these martyrs came, and on, and on. At length before this untiring perseverance, the granite bulwarks of paganism began to yield. The stronghold was carried, and the foundations of the new Empire firmly laid—an Empire, so immeasurably superior to the ancient one in its spirit, its extent, its duration.

The city now presents two aspects the decay and demolition of ancient Rome on the one hand, and the building up of the new Rome on the other.

Built amid the wreck and on the ruins of collapsing paganism, the new Rome presents the most perfect metamorphosis of worship. The change that has been wrought is complete and fundamental. There was nothing ever like it in the history of the world. The old Rome lingers on a while, but there is no amalgamation. A most dirtinct line of separation runs between the two. As the one disappears, the other expands and takes possession of the ground. Throughout this change, the original idea attaching to Rome as the earth's capital remains unchanged. She does continue to be mistress of a world, but by the grace of God mistress no longer of a heathen, but of a Christian world. The sway acquired by ancient Rome was but to foreshadow Rome's supernatural destiny in Christendom. The temporal power and wealth she had acquired, enabled Rome after her conversion to cast abroad among the nations the seeds of Christianity, and to leaven with the saving truths of the Gospel, the entire human family.

The Christian hierachy is, in all its essentials, of divine origin. But now in its accidental development, it adapted itself at once to the system of the imperial government. This system was ready to hand, practical, efficient, and easily understood by all.

God had now at last come to the relief of those who had so long and heroically witnessed for Him with their blood. He granted Constantine that glorious victory over the tyrant Maxentius which opens a new era in the history of Rome. The victorious army entered the city with the sign of the cross and the name of Jesus flaunting on their banners to the breeze. Senate and people went forth to welcome the conquerors. An arch of triumph was erected. In the inscription carved thereon, no mention was made of any heathen god. Constantine attributed the victory solely to the assistance of the One Most High God. On the inside of the arch were the words "To the Deliverer of the City—to the Peace-giver." For the first time in the eleven hundred years that Rome had stood, did a conqueror dare to forget Jupiter of the Capitol, and omit to lay at his feet the laurels that were won.

It was decreed that a statue should be erected by the city to the conqueror. Constantine gave orders that in lieu of the sceptre to be placed in its hands, a cross be substituted bearing the inscription:—

"In this saving sign, emblem of real strength, "have I delivered your city from thraldom and re- "stored glory to the senate and people."

At length by the grace of God,—the King of kings and Lord of lords, did the Christian religion, after a long and bloody struggle, the equal of which the world has never seen, come off victorious even in that very Rome which St. Peter had entered under such unfavorable circumstances. Those proud and haughty patricians prostrated themselves in low humility before the cross. It was the emblem of that freedom, which is freedom indeed, the signal that Christ had commenced to reign, that He triumphs and governs, even as this truth is proclaimed to the world to-day by the granite tongue of the great obelisk at St. Peter's. The new era begins.

XII.
THE VATICAN.

WHEN the persecutors were at length vanquished by the strong endurance of the persecuted, and the new Rome sprung into being, the first impulse to her new architectural embellishment was given by that feeling of deep reverence for St. Peter which had been transmitted from generation to generation. That Vatican hill 'neath which his precious remains had lain so long, was now consecrated to his memory and selected as the abode of his successor.

The Vatican is to Christian Rome, what the Capitol was to pagan Rome. It is the central, the principal point of the city. This hill derives its name from an obscure little town called Vaticum that stood there prior to the founding of the city. It obtained its celebrity as the ground whereon the martyrs suffered, wherein their bones were laid, and on which now stands the great Basilica of the Prince of the Apostles, as well as the palace of his successor. By reason of all these circumstances the Vatican is become synonymous with the Holy See, and symbolical of that See's supreme authority.

Constantine, after winning that battle which was fought near the gates of Rome under the new cross-bearing standards, resolved in thanksgiving to the Redeemer to build several Christian temples in different parts of the city. The greatest of all these was to be that dedicated to St. Peter. The Vatican was chosen for its site.

St. Sylvester, the first of Peter's followers who governed the Church in peace, went in solemn procession to the Vatican hill to lay the foundation stone of the new temple. The undisturbed foundations of Nero's circus, a spot on which such a countless number of Christians had shed their blood for the faith, served as a foundation for three sides of the new Basilica. No place, thought St. Sylvester, could be more appropriately chosen for God's worship than that hallowed by the blood of so many martyrs. Constantine himself was present at this solemn ceremony. He was without his crown, and desired to cast up the first shovel of earth with his own hands. Tradition says that on this occasion he laid aside his robe of state, and in honor of the twelve Apostles carried twelve hampers of earth on his own shoulders.

The old basilica, with its five naves and hundred columns, was much more like the present St. Peter's than is generally known. This may be seen by the description given of it by St. Paulinus in his letter to Pammachius. Before the entrance stood the atrium girt all round with pillars. A flight of broad marble steps led up to the gate. On the platform of these steps the successor of St. Peter was wont to receive the successor of Augustus, when the German Kaiser went to receive the imperial crown at the hands of the Pope and to pray at the tomb of the Apostles. In the building of the basilica the "Witness"—the CONFESSIO, or grot in which were the remains of St. Peter, was the all important point which determined the several parts of the entire structure. This grotto was divided into two compartments, the upper and the lower. In the latter the body of the Saint was laid with great solemnity in an immoveable coffin which was afterward encased in a massive richly-guilt capsule of bronze. By this capsule is an altar. Over the "Confession" at the intersection of the centre-lines of the great cross-naves, that is, immediately under the cross that surmounted the dome, was erected the high altar. To the "Confession" a double flight of gentle steps led down. These steps were of beautiful white marble, and the floor beneath was covered with costly stones. A balustrade of white marble on which eighty-nine lamps hung burning night and day ran round the "Confessional" or "Confessio."

With this church and with the scarce less beautiful basilica of the Lateran, began the monumental architecture of the new city. The demolition of heathen Rome went on daily faster and faster by the conversion of pagan monuments into Christian ones. The building of the new basilica progressed rapidly, and at length high in air upon its gable was raised the sign of Redemption. As the wondering pagans paused beneath the beautiful columnade to admire the edifice, they might say to themselves:— "Lo! within that basilica in a rich vault and golden shrine, is the highly venerated body of a Jewish fisherman, who from his lake of Galilee came to Rome at the time of Claudius or Nero." The circus was torn down. Its vast ruins which had supplied stone for the basilica presented now the dreary aspect of a quarry. By the Christians this building of the basilica on, and of, the ruins of the heathen circus was interpreted the victory of the Christian faith over pagan worship.

XIII

THE BRONZE STATUE OF ST. PETER.

There is at St. Peter's a very ancient bronze statue of the Apostle in which he is represented in a sitting posture with his right hand raised in the act of blessing, and holding the typical keys in his left.

This statue deserves a brief notice on account of its very singular history. It occupies at present a very conspicuous place in the basilica, but formerly stood in a little chapel hard by. Though another very ancient statue of St. Peter was in Rome, and indeed is there still, the one we speak of, engrossed all the veneration of the Romans. It was looked upon as yielding a special protection to them and to their city. To this, they invariably had recourse in their troubles. As devotion to this statue increased, it was thought proper to give it a prominent and roomly site in the great church itself. There it has been for centuries, and from the kisses bestowed on it by the millions of pilgrims that visit St. Peter's, the metal of the forward foot is noticeably worn away.

According to reliable documents still preserved at the Vatican, Pope Leo the Great, had this statue cast on his return to Rome after his interview with Attila. Tradition clothes that historic event with its own imagery. The sight of the Venerable Leo coming as mediator for the city made, it is said, a deep impression on the barbarian. But, it is added, it was not Leo alone he saw before him. Behind the imploring Pope, Attila beheld a supernatural personage in the form of a majestic venerable and elderly man, clad in episcopal robes, who threatened him with death if he denied the petitioner's request. Tradition says it was St. Peter who thus appeared to save and succor the city in its need.

Whatever degree of importance we may attach to this tradition, it is at any rate historically true that Attila, who had till then without fear or ruth scattered devastation 'round him by fire and sword, turned suddenly back after this interview with Leo, abandoned his declared purpose of going to Rome, and hastened to return to Pannonia. In Leo's own time the Romans began to keep the sixth of June—the day of his interview with the Hun as a festival in honor of their delivery. It is thought that in thanksgiving for the protection afforded on that occasion to the city by St. Peter, Leo had the statue of Jupiter which had long stood in the Capitol, recast into one of the Apostle, as the guardian of Rome. Several antiquarians are indeed of opinion that the present statue is the very statue of Jupiter itself, merely with other head and hands. The chief reason assigned is that this one does not even remotely resemble any other statue of the Saint. This is thrown up to us as a matter of reproach. But even supposing it were so, we can see nothing wrong in the matter. Let no change at all be made, could not the statue of Jupiter be blessed and consecrated to St. Peter just as pagan temples were converted into Christian ones? But it is all false. If the old statue merely got, as is suggested, a new head and new arms, there certainly should remain some sign of the jointure. Not a trace of anything of the kind however is to be found. Of the old Jupiter statue then nothing now remains but the metal moulded anew into that we have of St. Peter. The statue is in a sitting posture on a marble chair, and the ground on which it rests is now covered with green porphyry slabs. In the ninth century this ground or upper part of the pedestal was covered with plates of gold bearing an inscription in Greek. Mabillon recovered the inscription and published it from a valuable manuscript of Roman Epigraphy and Topography found in the library of Einsiedeln. The copy of this inscription taken by the anonymous compiler of the Einsiedeln Code is very faulty. The following is an attempt at a translation:—

> "God the Word beholds on gold
> The Rock divinely hewn:
> Firm on this, I falter not."

There is a great deal about this monument worth remarking. There it stands, made of the identical brass that composed the Jupiter of the Capitol. Jupiter was the symbol of warlike Rome, ruling the world by the terror of his arms. The Fisherman of Galilee ruling the regenerated world by the power of faith and love, is the emblem of Christian Rome. On the one, was the haughty toga, on the other are priestly vestments. Jupiter grasped the thunderbolt, Peter's hand is raised in the act to bless. We may also notice the circumstances under which the modern statue was erected. The fierce Attila, the scourge of mankind, was softened and turned back to Pannonia by Pope Leo. One of Leo's successors, five hundred years later, is seen sending the crown which he has blessed to Attila's Christian successor. That statue of Peter is subsequently venerated by all nations. The conquerors Belisarius and Totila respect it, and Charlemagne bows down beneath that hand lifted to bless. Pilgrims from the most distant parts of Christendom, kings and queens as well as peasants, all came to venerate and devoutly kiss the statue of him who has taken the place of Jove in the Christian Capitol. The statue had its enemies also. It is to this, Leo the Iconoclast alludes in his letter to Gregory II:—"I will send to Rome also and have the bronze statue of the Apostle Peter pulled down." To which the Pope replies: "If you send troops to Rome to tear down the statue of St. Peter, we would have you bear in mind that we shall hold ourselves guiltless of the blood that may be shed on the occasion: be it upon your head." Then came the Lombards who for two hundred years menaced the city and statue of the Apostle, and the thousand petty rulers that rose and fell in quick succession in Italy. This statue was particularly obnoxious to all those who hated the Christian name and Christian Rome. Thus we see the Statue like the Holy See always had its enemies as well as worshippers.

XIV.

THE CITY OF THE CÆSARS BECOME THE CITY OF THE POPES.

THE particular motive which induced Constantine to give up Rome as the capital of the empire and transport his court to Byzantium has never transpired. No historian informs us what it was. The feeling at the time grew general that the sway of the Cæsars in Rome had come to an end, and perhaps this, and the knowledge Constantine had that the spiritual empire whose prince he had recognized in Pope Sylvester, should far outstretch and overshadow the temporal, moved him to the step. At any rate, the finger of God is evidently discernible in the event.

Henceforward the Popes are the only persons who appear to watch over the well-being of Rome. All that the successors of Constantine did for the city, was to rob her of her monuments. Constantine called his capital on the Bosphorus "New Rome," and had transported thither any quantity of metal and marble statues, with works of art of all description. His object was to make his "New Rome" as like the old one as possible, and, if possible, to make it outrival her in beauty and magnificence. Accordingly, at immense trouble and expense, he had among other things the Palladium transported thither, together with a beautiful monolythe column of porphyry a hundred feet in length, which he set up in the Byzantine forum.

Henceforth we see the Christian element entirely prevail at Rome. Her Palladium are the bones of the Apostles and martyrs which repose in the Vatican and Callistine catacombs. Here also lie the remains of all St. Peter's successors, encircled with a halo of glory derived from their many virtues and the sanctity of their lives, such as no other dynasty on earth can boast.

Thus the Popes are now the only ones who maintain the majesty of the city. The city of the Cæsars is a wreck. It is being levelled by the successors of Augustus. The Popes alone arrest the work of ruin. They adopt into the "Eternal City" of St. Peter, the monuments of ancient Roman art and splendor. A word now on a few of these monuments.

The wooden temple of Jupiter on the Capitol is called to-day the "Altar of Heaven," *Ara Cœli*. It is consecrated to the divine child descending from heaven, and born into the world on that night of grace and good-will to men. On the Feast of the Nativity the Saviour-Child is here represented in a crypt with a statue of Augustus on one side, and a statue of the Sybil on the other, in remembrance of a vision which Augustus is said to have had in that place of a god-like child with whom he, the world's conqueror, as announced by the Sybil, should one day share his empire. The oracle is fulfilled. The Capitol, the symbol of an all-devouring ambition and lust of power that lorded it ruthlessly over the heathen world, is now, in the form of an infant, become the emblem of all that is tender and loveable upon earth, bringing tidings of salvation and freedom to the nations. The frowning majesty of the ancient Capitol is exchanged for the winning sweetness of the new-born Child, the Saviour. The priests of the Capitol are now the lowly sons of St. Francis, who minister in the *Ara Cœli*, and whose voice bearing tidings of deliverance to the nations, is heard beyond the utmost limits of the ancient empire.

This regeneration, however, of the memorable spots and monuments of the ancient city, is not without its exceptions. The Palatine whereon Romulus first pitched his hut, and which was afterwards defiled by the orgies of Nero, has so far, it would seem, resisted all renovation. Nothing since would thrive there. In the course of time, many attemps were made to settle it; dwellings, convents, monasteries, palaces, were put up. But it was only to heap ruins on ruins, and make the place look more blighted than before. Nature in its wildest state of thorn, briar, and thistle, has taken possession of those grounds of folly and luxury. Here and there in the wild wilderness, you may observe a patch of lettuce or of vines. But they are like oases in the dreary waste of this rank and noxious vegetation. For a long period the ruins of the Palatine served as a quarry for the building of palaces and churches in the city. At the very foot of the hill, there is now a small monastery of the Seraphic St. Bonaventure, as if to contrast forcibly the blessed poverty of Christianity with the most extravagant luxury the world ever witnessed. In the garden of this cloister is seen the only generous produce of this soil—a luxuriant palm. All else on the Palatine is a wild waste of ruin and desolation. Of this hill, nothing remains to the modern world but the word "palace," which, derived from the magnificent dwellings that once stood on the Palatine, has passed into all the languages of Europe.

The famous Pantheon met a better fate. The temple of all the gods is the only great monument of pagan Rome, that now exists in a state of complete preservation. Here it was, in this Roman temple of all gods, that sin and error held most sway. It was not thundering Jove alone who was here enthroned, nor the austere Juno, as conceived by the early Romans, but also Venus and Pandemos. When Rome in the zenith of her power erected this temple, she betrayed a falling off from her early virtue, and made a misuse of her noble gifts. The Pantheon was the brand of her degeneracy. That city, which had attained a pitch of greatness and glory such as the world had never seen, which was unique in the world's history, and in every way calculated to produce on the nations, an impression of her high and solemn majesty, mistook her calling and exhibited thenceforward a picture of corruption and iniquity that was never witnessed since the flood, and scarce surpassed by the crimes of ancient Babylon. This Pantheon, the symbol of Rome's consecration of herself to every vice and error, after lying a ruin for several centuries, was finally dedicated to the one true God in honor of all the

Christian martyrs, and is now the symbol of the city's consecration to the Most High. On the high altar, Mary is enthroned as queen of martyrs. The Pantheon is thus sanctified to-day, and is filled with the majesty of God and the glory of His saints. Its wonderful architecture obtained its fullest expression, and was converted to the noblest use, when a copy of the whole structure with its wonderous dome, was raised in mid air upon St. Peter's, the world's cathedral. On the frieze running round the whole circumference, is the following inscription in mosaic: "*Tu es Petrus et super hanc petram ædificabo ecclesiam meam, et tibi dabo claves regni cœlorum.*" The letters are six feet in length.

Where stood the baths of Domiti..n, is now the Church of Sts. Sylvester and Martin. It was built by Pope Sylvester, whose name it bears. Here he had long dwelt with a priest named Equitius prior to his flight to the solitary hill "Monte Soracte" in the Sabine swamp. It was in this church the successor of St. Peter approved, in 326, the decisions of the council of Nice, respecting the Divinity of Christ, reverently citing the noble words of St. Peter "Thou art Christ, the son of the living God." There, is also to be seen the remains of a mosaic representation of the Mother of God, that was put up by Pope Sylvester in honor of Mary "the Joy of Christians"— *gaudium Christianorum*—on the cessation of the persecution.

As time wore on, the transformation of the heathen into the Christian city progressed. It was now the capital of a new empire,—the empire of Christendom. The general face of things continued to alter more and more, in accordance with this high destiny. Peter, not Cæsar, rules at Rome, and, as Cæsar once was the all-in-all in Rome, so is Peter now. His church is the loftiest and the grandest in Christendom. The city is but that Church's atrium, and the Pope is the life and soul of Church and city.

XV.

ROME THE CENTRE OF THE CHRISTIAN WORLD.

WE cannot exaggerate the historic importance of the transformation that went on at this period. The old collapsing heathen city was silently transformed into the capital of the vigorous and conquest-bent empire of Christianity. When the deluge of northern barbarism rolled down upon Europe at the fall of the Western empire, overwhelming in its wild rush the other cities and towns of Europe, merging them all in its turbid waters and quenching all the lights of literature and civilization, Rome, like a second Ararat, proudly topped the flood and continued to afford a resting place to affrighted science and civilization. Herein was unquestionably the finger of God. Rome purified in the blood of her martyrs, and refreshed by drinking at the pure sources of faith, was designed by God to afford during this awful period, a firm and safe footing to St. Peter's successor.

In Christ's kingdom upon earth, the Pope holds the place of his divine Master. As Christ is king and ruler, the Pope is king and ruler. Christ's kingdom is not indeed of this world. But then, it is in this world, and so its chief must needs have a dwelling place on earth whence he may govern that kingdom without interference. Christ appointed Peter His vice-gerent. As chief of Christ's flock, Peter fixed his see in Rome. Rome thus became the first see of the Christian world. Not through any merits of her own, does Rome hold this precedence. Her pre-eminence is due solely to the merits, or rather to the divine election, of him who was her first bishop. This precedence of Rome then is really a personal thing. It is an honor attaching to the Primate or chief bishop of the Church. Though personal however in that sense, it is not given for the individual's sake. It was conferred on Peter for the good of the entire Church, and thus also the precedence that Rome enjoys as the See of Peter, was given her not for her sake alone, but for that of all Christendom. It should not, of course, be thought that Rome was made the capital of Christendom because she was the chief city of the empire. To Peter, and Peter alone, she owes her supremacy, and through Peter she aims as of old, but in a different manner, as also indeed for a different end, to subdue all the nations of the earth. This, her destiny through Peter, is one she could not receive from a vote in the forum, a placet of the senate, or the fiat of a Cæsar. St. Peter's choice of Rome under the divine guidance, his ministry and his death in that city, are the events which determined the future of Rome. From these events she has received her high privileges and sublime destiny. She is the centre,—the capital of the whole Catholic world, and to this high destiny of Rome, all local interests whatsoever must ever remain subordinate.

In all its essential elements, the hierarchy was established by Christ, or formed at His immediate bidding. With Rome for a centre this hierarchy went at once into full working order. The practical wisdom of the Romans for administration, soon developed the existing groundwork into a complete and beautiful system. The empire of the Cæsars, as in all else, so in this, was but a preparation for the empire of Peter. The general organization and most of the details of the former, suited the latter, and were, accordingly, adopted. Cardinals and bishops form the Senate of Peter. The provinces send their bishops and archbishops to the States-Council,—the synods and general councils: vice-gerents in provinces, or portions of provinces, are the patriarchs and archbishops. Monasteries and convents may be compared to the old colonies that became, wherever they were established, so many centers of material and intellectual improvement. The ambassadors of Peter's successor go forth in all directions. They pass far beyond the extremities of the old imperial roads, bearing embassies of the divine truth,—holiness of life and pure worship. The traces of the old imperial regime were still everywhere visible, and, through the channels which the old iron sway had cut into society, now flowed forth the waters of life to the provinces—to the world—from Rome.

Peter's ambassadors were sent to all the nations of the earth, and, to all the nations of the earth, they found their way. Rome's spiritual sway over mankind was infinitely more complete than ever was the material sway of the Cæsars. Peoples and tribes who had never heard of Rome before, now learned her name and her history, because thence had come their first spiritual fathers. Even in those places where the name of Rome had resounded in men's ears for centuries, the word now gained in majesty and significance. For centuries this "Roma" has been the mother and governess of the nations. They thronged round her to gather the pure words of life from her lips. She treasured up for them, besides, and dealt out with unsparing hand all that remained of ancient literature and civilization. By means of these charitable institutions of the Church,—the religious orders,—the successor of St. Peter could act the good Samaritan by Europe. He was enabled to play the part of the generous philanthropist who, mid the horrid scenes of a city devoted to pillage and destruction, picks up a helpless child, and acts by it as a father.

The nations of Christendom, under the Christian law given them by Papal Rome, of faith, hope and charity, were formed to godliness and incited to strive after the Christian ideal in their social relations. In return for the good he wrought, the successor of St. Peter was looked up to by all Christendom with filial and heartfelt affection.

XVI.
THE PATRIMONY OF ST. PETER.

The local church of the city of Rome was possessed of considerable ecclesiastical property, long before she was endowed by Constantine. The revenues of this property were employed for the repairing and building of churches, furnishing the altar, and the support of the clergy and the poor. Not the wants of Rome alone were thought of. The Romans frequently sent assistance to other churches in Italy, Greece, Asia-Minor and Palestine. This revenue all passed through the Pope's hands. It went by the name of the "Patrimony of St. Peter," so that through these charitable works, the Pope, as St. Ignatius who was martyred A. D. 106, expresses it, seemed to hold "a presidency of charity," and this, not only as regards Rome, but also all other churches.

With regard to charitable foundations and institutions, the seed sown at Rome by the Apostle was not fruitless. The Romans readily comprehended that love of our neighbor is a proof, and a prop of that charity, without which there is no salvation, as well as a bond of union among the faithful. The rich were taught, that to be saved, they must be charitable; that their bounty to the poor would be the measure of their glory. As Peter wrote to the faithful of Asia-Minor, and admonished them to love each other with a pure heart, to be compassionate, brotherly, kind and generous; so did he teach his Christians at Rome to practice that charity, by which every one should know they were Christ's disciples. The same doctrine is inculcated by Peter's successors. St. Clement writes:—"Who can estimate the value of charity? who can measure the height to which, through union with God, it elevates man?" This charitable spirit of the Romans had, at a very early day, put the Church in possession of considerable means,—the "patrimony of Peter,"—which, even in a worldly point of view, gave the see of Rome extraordinary importance. It acquired stability thereby, and the Pope, that position of freedom and independence so necessary in his case. Through the wealth at his disposal, in pure cash, vessels of gold and silver, and real estate, he commanded an influence not to be dispised. Add to this, the well-ordered graduating hierarchy, by which the Pope's influence was extended through and through the Church, and the fact that the decrees of synods and councils had to be submitted for his approbation, and it will be easy to understand what the supreme jurisdiction of the see of Peter meant even in those early and troublous times. Alexander Severus decided a law-suit, respecting a piece of property, in favor of the Roman Church. He viewed her as a standing corporate body, and takes occasion to praise her organization, especially in what regards the election of bishops. This, he thinks, were well worthy of imitation in electing officers for the imperial administration. The emperor Aurelian, though an enemy and persecutor of the Church, recognized the supremacy of the Pope over all the Christians of the empire. The catacombs were not the only places where the Christians assembled. They had many houses in the city wherein they ventured to meet, as the fury of persecution lulled. These houses were sometimes richly furnished, and generally possessed a great many silver lamps. When the persecution of Diocletian broke out, there were forty such houses in the city, although only the small space of thirty years had elapsed since that under Aurelian had ceased.

By an edict of Constantine, the right of the Church as a corporate body was formally recognized. Thenceforward donations of real estate to the Holy See came not only from Rome and the immediate environs, but also from distant parts of Italy, from Sicily, Corsica, Gaul, Syria, Asia-Minor and Egypt. The "Patrimony of St. Peter" was thus increased, and increased for the benefit of the entire world. In the desolation and distress, which accompanied the dissolution of the Western empire, not only had the Popes on many occasions, to provide for the needs of distant churches, but often for the wants of a whole province. Rome itself was a model to all other cities and churches as regards the establishment of charitable institutions. She provided hospitals for the sick, and homes for the aged poor, the widow, and the orphan. By this means, the Pope acquired almost complete independence of the now spent and tottering regime of the old empire, even before his more perfect and sovereign independence was secured for the good of Christendom by the acquisition of the States of the Church.

Regarding the administration of this heritage of St. Peter, the reign of Gregory the Great, merits some particular notice. Possessing a good practical knowledge of agriculture, he introduced everywhere through his dominions the best systems of tillage and farming that were then known, and showed the inhabitants how to increase the produce of their lands. Nothing escaped his notice. Not the smallest details of government does this truly great man deem beneath his attention. One sees that in these seeming trifles, as in the weightiest of his affairs, Gregory is actuated solely by his strong love of justice and the all embracing charity of his noble soul. To the peasantry, in particular, who, when just rescued from the claws of the Byzantine taxation, fell into the hands of the plundering conquerors of the empire, Gregory shows himself a lenient and kind ruler. He knows also how to protect his own rights against the encroachments of the violent princes of his time. Of his own ease and comfort, he took little thought. It could be said of Gregory that he was as poor as a monk, and as rich as a king. His income was great, and with it he was liberal to all needs save his own. He is often astonished himself at the wonderful bounty of God in providing the supplies for his liberality, and can scarce comprehend how it is the Church of Rome, that had to suffer her own share in the general distress, can, nevertheless, contribute so much towards the support of the clergy, the convents, the poor and the infirm, as also to provide for many who had been stripped of their all by the devastating armies. Besides all this, Rome had to furnish heavy contributions on several occasions to stay the fury of the victorious Lombards.

The states of the Church many a time aroused the jealousy and the avarice of the barbarians who commanded in Northern Italy. In all their attempts however at seizure and annexation, they strove, then as now, to justify by some title or other their acts of lawless violence and plunder.

XVII.

THE SUCCESSOR OF ST. PETER PROTECTOR OF THE CITY AGAINST THE BYZANTINE EMPEROR AND THE SUBALPINE BARBARIANS.

THE Eastern emperors through ambition and avarice, and the barbarians of Northern Italy, through mere lust of plunder and conquest, sorely harassed Rome for the next two centuries. The Lombards moved again and again upon the city. It was saved on such occasions, not by the distant emperor or his powerless exarchate, but invariably by the influence or mediation of the Popes. The Lombards, half-heathen Arians, thought that by exterminating the Roman Church, they could establish and insure their own sway over the entire of Italy. They fancied that the Popes favored the rule and policy of Constantinople, and were, consequently, hostile to themselves. On the other hand the Greek emperors oppressed the bishops of Rome because the latter would not openly espouse the imperial policy. When the Popes took it on themselves to do for the city or the province, what the exarchate either through carelessness would not, or through inability could not, effect, they were invariably accused of trespassing on the emperor's rights. The successors of Constantine must have begun to feel at this period, that God had, in the successors of St. Peter, raised up that strong arm, which, with firm grasp, was soon to take the helm of Italian and Roman affairs out of their own feeble hands. Men's minds were all turning to Rome not only as the source of pure faith and the fount of science, but also the model of society. It was impossible that such a city thus looked up to, could long remain the provincial town of a distant, effete and dissolute empire.

From Gregory the Great to Stephen III., who called the Franks to his assistance into Italy, a period of nearly one hundred and fifty years intervened. It was a period of fearful anarchy throughout all Italy, and its history is but very imperfectly known. The Eastern emperor continued to maintain some footing in the country, but indeed little more. His feeble rule was now limited to a portion of the coast near Ancona, and the duchies of Rome and of Naples. The kingdom of the Lombards which occupied nearly the whole of Italy, and was divided from North to South into two parts that were but loosely connected with each other, had no natural frontiers, nor indeed any very settled ones of any kind. Italy thus became the theatre of the continual wars waged by the semi-barbarous Lombards. She suffered all the horrors of the cruelty and devastation in which that fierce race seemed delighted to indulge. In one of the later wars, the Lombards, baffled in their efforts to get possession of the city, wasted the whole surrounding country in such a frightful manner, that from that terrible destruction ensued the irreclaimable condition of those unhealthy desolate marshes of the Roman Campagna.

Rome, Ravenna, and Pavia were now the principal cities in Italy. Pavia was the Lombard capital; Ravenna was the seat of the Greek exarch. He ruled as a military despot. By his exactions, he kept the inhabitants in a state of chronic rebellion. A Greek commandant was still maintained in Rome, but his command was in reality but a nominal one.

From the beginning of the eighth century a desire for self-government began to agitate the Italians, especially those who were still subjects of the emperor. It was easy to see that the Byzantine rule in Italy was near its end. The Popes were often the only ones who acknowledged the actual government of the emperor. But the Popes were also in the eyes of the Italians the representatives, as well as the upholders of the old commonwealth. The Italians loved to think Rome was still the old republic. The idea was perhaps as faint as it was unreal, but such as it was, it fired Italian souls a little. In Rome the "Republic" would seem to mean at one time the neighboring territory that had not been seized by the Lombards, at another, the Greek exarchate with its five cities. The Popes looked on themselves and acted, as the defenders and protectors of the Roman commonwealth. What chiefly contributed to the great political power which the successors of St. Peter exercised at this period was the extraordinary religious veneration in which they were held by those barbarian tribes lately converted to Christianity, especially the Franks. This feeling was also very lively among the old-Italians, descendants of the early Christians. To this, must be added the large income of the "Patrimony" at their disposal. With no itching hands or selfish spirit was this "patrimony" liberally expended for the benefit of the people. Thus all Italians or "Romans" came to look on the successor of Peter as their natural ruler, as their defender and their protector against all comers. Nevertheless the Pope himself remained under nominal subjection to a distant sovereign power. He was, however, notwithstanding this fact, what Cæsar never could have been to all those who dwelt in the territory of the fancied "Roman Republic." Indeed, the emperors seemed now bent on treating their Italian possessions as a retreating army would a province they were compelled to abandon. All that could be done to strip and exasperate the inhabitants, was done. Meantime the Pope's conduct towards both sides,— the oppressed and the oppressors,—was ever soothing and conciliating. Thus the successor of St. Peter, through all change and circumstance, was becoming every year more fondly dear to the Italian people and twining himself more closely with their affections and aspirations. He thereby all the more securely assured himself of that independence, which as head of the Church he must necessarily possess.

But in that long and troublous period that elapsed between the arrival of the Lombards and the final attainment of independent sovereign authority by the Popes, the ideal "Republic" of the

Romans was more than once in extreme danger of being crushed to powder as between two millstones, by the Byzantine power on the one side, and the Lombards on the other.

XVIII

DEVELOPMENT OF THE POPE'S POLITICAL POSITION INTO INDEPENDENT SOVEREIGNTY.

The eighth century brought with it events which soon led to a crisis in the affairs of Italy. After the death of Justinian II., his murderer, Philippikus Bardanes, ascended the throne of Constantinople. It was customary for the Greek emperor at his accession, to send the Pope his confession of faith. Philippikus sent his, but it was openly monothelistical. It was, of course, rejected by the Pope and Roman clergy. The people were incensed; they caused large paintings of the six general councils to be made and had them hung round the walls of St. Peter's. This was intended as a political demonstration against the heretical emperor. The whole populace rose up against him. The nobility, the army, and the different guilds of the city, unanimously resolved to shake off his yoke. The people declared they would never acknowledge the new vice-gerent sent to Rome by the heretical emperor. A tumult ensued on the Via Sacra. A number of the Roman clergy went forth and separated the combatants. But the disturbance continued, and notwithstanding the efforts of Pope and clergy, this anarchical condition of affairs lasted upwards of a year and a half.

The revolt was not confined to the city alone. It spread far and wide through the Greek dominions. In the year 715, Pope Constantine died. He was a worthy predecessor of the great men that succeeded him in the chair of Peter, Gregory II., Gregory III. and Zachary.

As Gregory the Great had the faith borne to the distant country of the Anglo-Saxons, England, so did Gregory II. draw Germany, then covered with wood and swamp, out of the darkness of paganism, to the light of faith and civilization. In November 723, he raised St. Boniface to the episcopal dignity in Germany. These were gloomy days for Europe. Within, lawlessness, strife and bloodshed everywhere; while without, she was attacked on all sides, by the deadliest foes of Christianity, the Mussulmans. These were already masters of Spain and Portugal. They were fast moving upon France. Their fleets scoured the Mediterranean. Italy and Rome were threatened from the sea, and the inhabitants of the entire Peninsula watched in feverish anxiety the movements of the dreaded foe. Leo the Isaurian reigned on the Bosphorus. Leo was a mere military upstart, a man of no culture, with manners rude and coarse. He was a bold and able warrior, but had no taste whatever for the arts of peace. When emperor, he was seized with the Greek mania for theological disputes, and entered upon the discussion of matters of which he absolutely knew nothing at all. Besides, his mind was wholly unfit for such speculative argumentation. But it was on this very account, that his meddling in such matters was all the more dangerous. In the year 876, Leo published an edict requiring that pictures and statues be forthwith removed from all the Christian churches of the empire. At this a storm of revolt burst over the length and breadth of his dominions. In many places the minions of the emperor, disregarding the feelings of the populace, undertook, conjointly with the heretics, to carry out the prescriptions of the edict. Churches were broken open, and the streets were strewed with the fragments of torn paintings and broken-up statues and mosaics. Leo sent his edict to Rome as well as elsewhere. It called forth from Gregory a dogmatical document, wherein he tells the emperor it does not belong to him to give commands in matters of faith, nor is he despotically going to do away with a venerable usage. Leo threatened to depose the Pope. At this the citizens of Rome and the whole population of the Pentapolis, the Venetians and the Calabrians, rose up as one man, and declared their intention to maintain the Pope against the emperor by force of arms. Leo sent a fleet to Rome. But it was basely arranged that before they should enter the Tiber, Gregory was to be despatched by assasins. The plot was defeated by the sudden illness of Spatharius Morinus, one of the wretches hired for the purpose. The enraged mob fell upon the other conspirators and cut them to pieces. Hearing of this, the exarch resolved to march an army upon Rome. But the entire Pentapolis was up in arms against the Greek. The Lombard settlers in Tuscany declared likewise for the Pope and seized the Salarian bridge. The Greeks were obliged to return, and so determined had the Italians become in the Pope's cause against the emperor, that they actually resolved to choose an emperor of their own, raise an army and march against Constantinople. The little success they had had, aroused the national spirit and made the men of the ideal "Republic" of the eighth century, fancy they were the stern old Romans of a thousand years ago. But the re-establishment of the empire in the West was a chimera. Gregory thus far had opposed the rebels, and continued to do so now. But with all his influence, he could not prevent the Romans declaring their city free from all allegiance to the emperor of Constantinople. Some say the Romans on this occasion proclaimed the city and its dependent territory a Republic, with the Pope at the head of the administration. This, however, we cannot vouch for.

The Pope used all his influence to appease the people. He exhorted them not to cut loose from the imperial government. He addressed letters to Leo full of paternal advice, but at the same time in a tone of lofty boldness and wholesome severity. "We must address you," he says, in one of them, "in a manner rather rude and unpolished, for you are rude and unpolished yourself." Then follows an explanation of the Catholic veneration of holy pictures, simple enough for a child to understand. He adds that the Italians showed that they did not think Leo's own statues and pictures worthy of their reverence, by trampling them under foot. It is on this occasion he mentions that statue of St. Peter of which we spoke in the XIII. chapter. In a second letter Gregory enters at some length upon the question of the two powers, the spiritual and the temporal, the palace, as he calls it, and the Church. He points out the limits to the authority of each. The temporal prince, he says, in what regards the well-being of society can enforce his commands with the dungeon and the sword. The spiritual chief or first bishop employs no mater'al force, but punishes sinning souls with ecclesiastical censures, to the end that they may thereby be drawn from death to life in God. These documents are replete with noble and profound conceptions, and distinctly indicate the relations of Pope and Kaiser, of Church and State. This letter of Gregory's drew from the rough soldier a savage reply, wherein he says:—"I am Cæsar, and I am priest:" that is, I am State and Church, too. In the course of his answer to this, the Pope tells him: "Thy intellect and thy reasoning is that of a blunt unlettered soldier. Now, don't venture with such, upon an analysis of the dogmas of faith."

And thus was Italy lost forever to the imperial crown. True, several battles were afterwards fought between the Greek forces and the Lombards. In these wars the Pope was repeatedly called on for assistance and advice by the Greek commanders. But as a general thing, Rome took little part in these struggles. Though the city was still nominally under the emperor, the Romans practically disclaimed his rule. At length, Constantinople was forced to relinquish her hold on every foot of Italian soil. From within and from without, the Greek rule was equally attacked. Everything showed that a crisis in the political affairs of Italy was imminent. Some great change was inevitable. By degrees the Pope began to be regarded not only as the governor of Rome, but also of the whole Pentapolis. He was in fact looked up to as their chief by all those Italians in whatever part of Italy, who held to the ideal Republic. The next war of the Lombards hastened the march of events. Luitprand, one of the ablest of the Lombard kings, beleaguered and took Ravenna, the capital of the Byzantine government in Italy. He also became master of many of the towns and strongholds of Aemilia and the Pentapolis, and seized on Narni and Sutri in the Roman duchy. He prepared to march on Rome, but the Pope induced him by presents and persuasion to spare the city. Not only that, but so taken was Luitprand with the Pope, that he made him accept in the name of St. Peter, the town of Sutri. It was to be the private property of the Holy See. This was the first donation of a city to the Church, and thus Sutri may be said to be the germ of the Papal states.

Wars continued to be waged between the Greeks and Lombards for the soil of Italy. Fortune favored the Lombards. Encouraged by continual success, they at length resolved to make themselves masters of Rome. No secret was made of this resolution. The Romans were shaken with fear. Gregory II. and III. had indeed drawn a wall round the city, but this would not long protect it. The Pope turned in this extremity to the Franks for assistance. He created Pepin a Roman Patrician.

Under the Eastern emperors this was the highest dignity in the state. There was usually annexed thereto a certain amount of ecclesiastical patronage, and the patrician had some voice in many matters relating to the Church. On sending Pepin the dignity, the Pope addresses him as follows:—"Be thou the shield and sword of the Roman Republic throughout all Italy, and be especially the advowee of the Church." Such was the means of protection which the Pope devised for himself and the Romans. The dignity conferred on Pepin gave the brave Frank no right whatever to any power in Italy. It entitled him not so much as to hold possession of a single hamlet. The manner of the Pope's acting in this affair proves, that though he had not formally thrown off the yoke of the Cæsars, he yet looked upon himself as completely independent.

The attainment of sovereign independence at this period by the successor of St. Peter, was remarkably providential. There was, on one side, the Eastern empire crumbling to the dust. While the Greek could oppose no front to the onward march of victorious Islamism, he made the most ridiculous pretentions to a despotic interference in ecclesiastical affairs. In the West, on the contrary, there were the vigorous and warlike German nations. These were devoted heart and soul, to the Church and the Holy See. They were animated with all the impetuous zeal of recent converts. Between the two, the Popes, as champions of the great interests of the human race, occupied an independent and neutral ground, which they sought to isolate more and more from the conflicting interests of different nationalities. Thus were the states of the Church formed, and this their meaning in the world.

XIX.
ROME AS THE CAPITAL OF THE STATES OF THE CHURCH.

St. Peter had made Rome the capital of the Christian world. The liveliest reminiscences of the heroic days of Christianity, of the persecutions and the martyrs, were here preserved. Rome was the one city that reflected all the glories of the past. Politically, Rome was not even the chief city of the Greek exarchate in Italy. It was second to Ravenna in which was the seat of government. Rome was merely a town of the "subject Italian province." But as the Pope was the recognized protector of all that portion of Italy which did not acknowledge the Lombard sway, and as he was the acknowledged head of the ideal "Roman Republic," so Rome was always the capital of this ideal Italy which looked to the Pope as its chief ruler. It cannot be denied, however, that the Pope, at this period, possessed some rights not altogether imaginary over other towns and districts besides Rome and that Sutri, of which we spoke previously. When Pepin after defeating the Lombards in Italy made the famous "gift" to the Pope, he did so, not so much by way of donation as of restoration. In the council of state which he held with his nobles at Quercy, Pepin bound himself to see that the districts seized by the Lombards should be "given back" to the Holy See.

In another document, we find the Pope demanding the cities and lands belonging to the See of Peter from the king of the Franks, who, he says "holds his own crown by a decision of the bishop of Rome." This "giving back" must in all likelihood mean that now the Pope took regular possession as rightful ruler of those cities and districts, which had long looked upon him as their natural head and protector, and which indeed he had heretofore shielded and provided for with all the means and influence he could command.

The territory then given to the Pope, comprised the exarchate of Ravenna, the five cities, Rimini, Pesaro, Fano, Umana and Ancona, together with the town of Narni. Of Rome and the Roman duchy no mention is made. Perhaps it is because this territory had not to be conquered back from the Lombards. Nevertheless we find Pepin in the year 757, formally obliging the Romans to acknowledge the rule of the Pope, and exacting an oath of allegiance to the Pontiff. We do not stop to ask whether the Pope was justified in assuming the supreme rule of these provinces. They were long since completely lost to the Greek, and the emperor by abandoning them, had renounced all claim to any further possession.

Thus did the successor of St. Peter become the regular sovereign of the States of the Church with Rome for their capital, and these States being the property, the demesne, the "patrimony" of St. Peter, belong not to any Pope as an individual nor to any family or faction, but to the entire Catholic Church.

Let us now glance for an instant at the whole

chain of events that led to the establishment of the Papal rule. The independence which was thus secured the Pope is intimately connected with the role which the Papacy was destined to play in the world's history. Both were decreed and appointed by God, and both were given by Him for the benefit of the human family. The Papacy was made the centre of Christian unity. It is the foundation of the Church of Christ. To this, and not to the donation of Pepin, or to any political ability or intrigue, do the successors of St. Peter owe their exaltation. The circumstances which immediately led to the supreme power and political independence of the Popes, were entirely without the range of political calculations. The weakness and folly of the Eastern emperors who could no longer hold their Italian dominions; the ambition and avarice which possessed the Lombard kings and made them think of taking Rome and making it the seat of their government in Italy; the rise of the great Carolovingian dynasty in France; the love and veneration with which the inhabitants of Rome and the neighboring districts regarded the Pope; as well as those circumstances which made them, for many a year previously, look up to him as their natural ruler;— it was to the providential combination of all these circumstances that the Popes owed the sovereign authority which they now acquired. The Most-High had wisely disposed all things for the purpose. There was no choice left the successor of St. Peter. He had to assume the supreme power. He did so. He raised Rome from her neglected decaying condition and made her the flourishing capital of a stable and vigorous monarchy. The Pope saved Rome from the pitiless rule of the half-savage Lombards, and the Popes have that honor, which is unique in the world's history, that they came into possession of their states without committing or participating in the least act of injustice. Even in this, as in all else, the Popes, true to the great calling of the Papacy, only furthered the well-being of society by acquiring to themselves a regal crown.

We have glanced at the ways of Providence in bringing about this independency of the Popes from the stand-point of the Papacy itself. The divine action is no less discernible, if we view the same event from the stand-point of the political condition of Europe at that period. It will appear evident to any one, that the Papacy was raised to a condition of sovereign independence, at the very time that it became absolutely necessary, for the preservation of Europe and civilization, that it should be such a power.

The successor of St. Peter being supreme head of the Church and Vicar of Christ upon earth, is of course obliged to watch over the affairs of the entire Church. His voice must be heard in all parts of the Christian world advising and admonishing, investigating and judging, binding and loosing. When the empire was the world,—*Universus orbis*—the Pope's voice could, in many ways, reach his most distant children, and, with a hierarchy disciplined after the model of the empire's strong system of centralization, the unity of the Church could be easily preserved. If the Pope had then a political superior, this superior was also ruler of the world. This made a great difference as we shall see. For when the empire fell, and Europe was parcelled out into several independent kingdoms, the relations of the Pope to the world were wholly altered. Were the Pope now to be subject to any one of these, it were to be feared the others would, with difficulty, be induced to acknowledge him in their territories as the common Father of the faithful. This, as we can easily comprehend, would be a fruitful source of schism, scandal and confusion in the Church. What befell the patriarchs of Constantinople would befall the Popes. The schismatic Greek and the schismatic Russian churches hold the same dogmas. In this they are but one Church. All were formerly governed by the patriarch of Constantinople; but as soon as the patriarch became a subject of the Sultan's dominions, the Russians would no longer acknowledge his supremacy. They would not admit as superior, one who was himself subject to the Turk.

It is easy to understand the political grounds on which the different rulers would reject the influence of a spiritual authority subject to a foreign power. The spiritual power to reach all and be admitted by all, must be itself politically independent. The states of the Church were quite sufficient to secure the absolute freedom of the Pope against the despotism of the Greeks, the Lombards, and all others, and at the same time as a political power, they were so insignificant that none could be jealous of their strength or influence. They simply sufficed for the independence of him who was to govern the entire Church, whose influence should be felt at once in all nations, without his being subject to any himself.

To govern the Catholic Church, implies to be in immediate relations with every Church of Christendom, and hold regular communication with the eight or nine hundred bishops that preside over these churches; to appoint those bishops, to watch over the deposit of faith, the teaching of sound doctrine and pure morality, to maintain ecclesiastical discipline, to decide on questions of faith, to prevent heresies creeping in, to uproot abuses, to further the spread of the gospel, and to send missionaries into every clime and country on the face of the earth for the purpose of propagating the Christian faith and inculcating the pure morality of our holy religion. Furthermore, the head of the Church must, through his legates, endeavor to preserve friendly relations with kings and princes and all manner of governments. He must strive to maintain and promote that union and cordial understanding between the two powers, so useful, if not necessary to the welfare of each. From a consideration of those few points, we can perhaps form some idea of what the government of the Catholic Church means and what the weighty and countless cares of the successor of St. Peter. From all this it is easy to comprehend why it was ordained in the providence of God, that at the fall of the empire, the Pope should be clothed with temporal sovereign power. It was the only means whereby his independence could be secured, and the Papacy play that part in the world's history for which it had been created.

This temporal power of the Pope, the slow growth of centuries, and manifestly raised up by God for the freedom of religion and the Church, was looked on by all the nations of Christendom as something sacred; and that man would be held guilty of sacrilege, who should, under any pretext, dare lay hands on any part of this "Patrimony of St. Peter."

XX.
THE PAPAL STATES IN A NEW PHASE.

FROM the time the Papal States took, as such, their place among the nations of Europe, until the year 800, the advowson of the Carolovingian dynasty had to be often brought into play. The successor of St. Peter had, on more than one occasion, to invoke the protection of the Franks against the encroachments of the Lombards. This lasted until, after a decisive battle, Charlemagne declared the Lombard rule at an end, and placed the crown of Lombardy on his own head. The continual alarm in which the Popes stood, all those years, on account of the proximity of such hostile neighbors as the Lombards, no doubt made the idea occur to some of them, that it would be well to confer some more honorable title on the protectors of their states. Leo III. acted upon this idea. On Christmas night, of the year 800, the great Frank who had so nobly defended Christendom against the caliphs of Spain, against the savage hordes of Hungaria and Sclavia, and against the obstinate valor of the Saxons in Northern Germany, Charlemagne, knelt at the tomb of the Apostles in St. Peter's basilica. As the solemnities were about to commence, the Vicar of Christ approached the kneeling monarch and solemnly placed the imperial crown upon his head. At this the people burst forth into the wildest acclamations, shouting: "Life and victory to the illustrious Charles, to him who is crowned by God, to the great and peace-giving emperor of the Romans!"

This Roman-German empire was quite a different thing from the old empire or that of Constantinople. The imperialism in this case was simply a thing of ecclesiastical institution. It was created for the Church's sake, and belonged to herself, as the states from which she gave the title. In this sense, there is the closest connection between the Kaiser and the Church. Charlemagne had already written to the Pope: "Thy cares are my cares and my cares are also thine." The illustrious Frank had now received a sacred character. Among all the princes of the earth, he was the first-born, the eldest son of the church. As such he was to be honored before all others. But in return, it became his duty before all others, to yield submission and pay reverence to his mother. Thus was the imperial dignity linked with the states of the Church.

Subsequent to this period, Europe presents a new order of things that may be designated the Christian-Germanic. The Holy See that was already the centre of Christianity in spirituals, now becomes also the centre of this new order in the political world. From this forward, we find the successor of St. Peter compelled more and more by the position of affairs, by the wishes and prayers and necessities of princes and peoples, by the force of general opinion, to take the place of umpire at the head of the European commonwealth, to declare, and see carried out, the Christian law of nations and to mediate between princes and people on all sides. The nations of Europe formed then only one commonwealth which history has called Christendom. Between them was the common bond of Christian baptism which makes all, princes and people, no matter what the form of government, one in Christ. No politician ever conceived any system of government better than that which was thus by God's providence, quietly brought about in Europe.

Rome, the city of the Galilean fisherman, the capital of a small territory, merely sufficient to secure the freedom of her ruler, was the legitimate source of the new imperialism. She was the metropolis of Christendom. In this character, she represents in a manner incomparably higher than ancient Romè, the idea of Catholicity. This Rome is true to her sublime destiny. She shelters the great High-Priest of the world from the annoyance or interference of any earthly power in the discharge of his divine duties, and gives free access to him to all the nations of the earth. This spiritual centre attracts within its influence the most Northern German tribes and peoples, as well as the whole Celtic race of Western Europe. In the East, the Sclaves and the Magyars submit to the gentle yoke, and barbarism disappears, as the spiritual power of Rome is extended. The Rome of the Cæsars anihilated nationalities, the Rome of St. Peter recognizes and props them up. In her eyes, Romans, Greeks, Germans, Celts, Sclaves, all are equal. She dispenses the blessings of religion to all alike, to the most distant and wretched, as well as to the most mighty and flourishing races. This Rome, calls herself even in the worldly order, the mother of the nations, and, thanks to her own neutrality, she is enabled to hold forth for their imitation, the grand fundamental ideas on which society should be based, that high, though perhaps unattainable ideal of perfect government, founded on the eternal ethical truth of God.

This idea of the perpetual neutrality of Rome is what preserved to the successor of St. Peter his peaceful possessions. The idea of a free Pope in his own independent principality is really a great and sublime one, and, even if the practical working be not up to the ideal, the latter is not the less sublime on that account. This ideal, in fact, was more than once, all but realized. Even to present the idea to society, and bring the nations to make efforts after its realization, was already a great stride on the way of progress and civilization. For this alone, had it never done ought else, were the erection of the Papacy into a temporal sovereignity an event of incalculable benefit to Europe. The state, which since the eleventh century, has been doing all this for Europe, and would have done so more effectually had princes and people better understood their own interest, should be prized as the apple of the eye. It would be so prized too, were not the sublime Christian political idea completely lost sight of. The Papal States with their high destiny, should be looked on as the embodiment of a divine principle which God Himself introduced into the world for the good of the human race.

Such were the Rome of St. Peter, the Rome that WOULD be, were it not for the infirmity of fallen man, and the old warfare waged by the wicked against God's kingdom on earth.

XXI.
THE PAPAL STATES IN THEIR RELATION TO ITALY.

WE have seen how, under the directing hand of God, a state was formed in Italy which bore in a particular manner upon the eternal destinies of the whole human family. This state secured for the head of the Church a position of perfect freedom and independence, and thereby made him in all political disputes and contentions whether among princes or nations, an unprejudiced referee.

We have said that the political independence of the Holy See was a necessary condition of the freedom of the Church. This political independence is, so far as we can trace the finger of God in history, part of the divine plan of the Church's position on earth. Its foundations were therefore laid from the earliest days of her existence. The fall of the empire was evidently the moment for the accomplishment of the divine design. The subjugation of the greater part of Italy by the hardy Ostro-Goths, imperilled the independence of the Papacy. Had these established themselves firmly on the soil of Italy, they would certainly take Rome for their capital. With this warlike and concentrated power once in strong possession, it were all over with the Papal States, and the freedom of Christ's Vicar. It would also come to pass, as we shall show hereafter, that the natural character of the Italians would completely disappear. But the hand of Providence was guiding events. The Goths who thus menaced the Papacy, disappeared themselves from history. After the victories of Narses, there was little immediate danger that a Gothic-Italian kingdom would interfere with the future of St. Peter's city. But neither was Constantinople to hold absolute sway over Rome. The "Eternal City" had fallen, under its rule, to the rank of a mere provincial town. True, the Greek emperor was himself far enough out of the Pope's way, but that state mechanism whereby Constantine had bound together the distant parts of his empire, could be used with effect by any of his successors who might feel so disposed, to crush the ecclesiastical authority of the bishop of Rome. The independent action of the Papacy was to be secured through the new order of things to be established in Europe. The Lombards came to Italy. They were a powerful people, yet not quite able to root out the Greeks. They could not drive the imperial troops off the soil nor consequently possess themselves of the entire peninsula. While both these parties were contending for the mastery, the Pope's position of political independence was quietly strengthened and, after a little time, permanently secured. We have before indicated the historical events which led to this consummation.

And now we may ask, how did this new condition of the Papacy—the political supremacy of the Popes—bear upon Italy? The Pope who is head of the Church is also an Italian prince. His duties towards the Church are, in no wise, incompatible with his obligations towards his subjects. As an Italian prince he loves his country and furthers her welfare; as Vicar of Christ and successor of St. Peter, he loves the Church and serves her as "Servant of the servants of God." This double love, this twofold duty go hand in hand, and each rather assists than obstructs the other. Where the earthly ruler can merely see his native land, the Pope sees native land and furthermore a portion of Christ's great kingdom of souls. The majorities of the Popes were Italians by birth. For centuries back, none but Italians are eligible. The Pope's supreme council, the College of Cardinals, are nearly all Italians. In like manner, the several courts for treating the general affairs of the Church, and the different Roman congregations are mainly composed of Italians. And lastly, Italians besides being the only ones eligible to the Chair of Peter, are generally preferred and, indeed, sometimes too exclusively, to all the dignities and emoluments of the Papal Court.

Between the decline of the old imperial rule and the rise of the great monarchies of modern times, Italy, with the Pope and his government in her midst, and with her other flourishing principalities, republics, and free cities, certainly had her day,—a day of dazzling glory and power, such as none of the sister nations of Europe has yet surpassed. The Italian nation, although not one centralized power, yet lived and moved with perfect freedom in accordance with the national tastes.

Political science reached a high degree of perfection in all the cities of Italy, and the most correct notions as to the best interests of communities, were arrived at in those little free republics. In military matters, both as to the bravery of the troops and the skill of the generals, the Italians ranked foremost in Europe. This flourishing Italy, however, was for a long time subject to the German Kaiser. But when the emperor abused his power to oppress the country, that Italy of the Popes—the States of the Church,—stood manfully up for its rights, and, if overpowered for a season, never rested till it had recovered either by diplomacy or the sword, its lost privileges or possessions. Without being part of a united Italy, it was national, it was catholic and, at the same time, an Italy of the Italians.

At the time the States of the Church took their place among the governments of Europe, the germs of these remarkable Italian nationalties were already commencing to develop. The successor of St. Peter, under whose protecting care they advanced to maturity, had indeed often sore need of more material power than what the small "Patrimony of St. Peter" could supply. He was often the only prince in Italy who dared make head against the Kaiser in defense of Italians and Italian rights. Still, such as she was, Italy owed her all to the Popes.

XXII.
THE SARACENS IN ITALY.

WE shall mention here only a few of the most important events that took place in Italy between the years 830 and 880. Storms burst over Italy within these fifty years that threatened the complete anihilation of Christian society.

The monarchy of Charlemagne had fallen to decrepitude. The king of the Franks, the eldest son and chosen adowee of the Church, had now his hands full to mind himself. Southern Italy fell into the hands of the Saracens. These had crossed from the coast of Africa, Candia, and Spain, thirsting for the conquest of the beautiful Italian peninsula. In the year 831, the crescent waved triumphantly over Sicily. The news that Palermo had fallen into the mussulman's hands and was become a seat of Saracen power, struck fear and horror into the hearts of the Romans. From the sea, the city was entirely open to the enemy. The old crumbling walls of Porto and Ostia would not check the grim foe for an hour, should the Caliph resolve to carry out his intentions of attacking Rome from the Tiber. With all haste, Pope Gregory IV. had the fortifications of the harbor repaired. He superintended the works in person. But the dissensions of the two dukes who held Southern Italy, gave the enemy an easy passage by land. The Caliph marched to Rome and plundered the two basilicas of the Apostles, Peter and Paul. But after some time spent before the walls, he had to draw off his troops without having effected an entrance into the city.

The enemy was gone, but the danger remained. St. Leo IV. succeeded Gregory. Leo's name ranks with the greatest of St. Peter's successors. He proved as competent a ruler in temporals, as he was in spiritual matters. In the presence of such fierce and powerful enemies, he managed to defend with surprising success, both the city and his States. Heretofore the Vatican and its adjoining grounds were not within the city proper. On this account St. Peter's fell an easy prey to the Saracens. Leo now extended the limits of the city so as to include the Vatican hill. This new portion of the city was called after his name. The harbor fortifications were not yet completed, when tidings reached Rome that an immense Saracen fleet was being fitted up for an attack on Rome by water. This was in 849. The Pope on receiving the intelligence called on Naples and Gaeta to send a few vessels to his assistance. They came under command of a young officer named Cæsarius, and had only just entered the mouth of the Tiber, when the Saracens hove in sight. Leo himself at the head of his troops hastened off to Ostia to meet the foe. It was a time of frightful anxiety for Rome and Italy.

Mid singing of hymns and psalms, Leo led his little army to the Church of St. Aurea in Ostia, and there confessed and administered holy communion to the soldiers. He then knelt and prayed:—"O God, Who supported the sinking Peter, and delivered Thy Apostle Paul when he was a third time shipwrecked, hear us, we beseech Thee, through the merits of both, and grant strength to the arms of these Thy faithful, who are about to do battle against the infidel enemies of Thy Church, to the end that in the victory Thy name may be glorified amongst all nations."

The Saracen sail appeared and an immense fleet rode up before Ostia. The Christians gave battle at once. They pressed their galleys eagerly forward to the fight. But a storm soon arose and separated the combatants in hopeless confusion. The enemy's ships were scattered in all directions. Most of them went to the bottom and the remainder were cast up disabled on the coast. The Saracen loss was tremendous. Numbers were killed in the battle, but many more perished by the fury of the elements. The survivors were taken in chains to Rome and put to work on the new Vatican fortifications. Thus the very hands that sought and fought to demolish Rome, are now compelled to add to her strength.

This battle before Ostia was the fitting prelude to that of Lepanto. The young Cæsarius was the worthy predecessor of the hero, Don Juan, and Leo IV. in the one, is what Pius V. is in the other. If the engagement before Ostia was not so magnificent in the display of forces, it was certainly as decisive of the fate of Italy. Raphael has left a painting of the battle scene which now hangs in the Vatican. The Romans long celebrated the commemoration of the victory, as one obtained of heaven through the intercession of the blessed Apostles Peter and Paul.

For some years after this battle, the Saracens left Rome alone. St. Nicholas I. was a prudent and competent prince, and maintained tranquillity both in the city and throughout his states. He was the first Pontiff who assumed the regal crown and was perhaps the ablest as well as the most fortunate occupant of the Chair of Peter since it was filled by the Great Gregory. Princes might take a lesson of him how to govern, while he was to ecclesiastics a model of apostolic zeal and sacerdotal virtue. Under St. Nicholas was brought into full light the great idea of the Christian Republic of nations, each working out within itself its own proper development, with the Holy See in the midst of all, advising, encouraging, judging, condemning, restraining.

His successor Adrian II. nobly upheld this high position. In the early part of his reign, however, he had several difficulties to encounter. The Roman aristocracy became impatient. The iron heel of the Cæsars was no longer there to bend their stiff necks. The nobles grew refractory and rebellious. They rose in arms against the Pope, but only succeeded in bringing dishonor and disgrace upon themselves. Before this trouble was entirely allayed, Adrian died. In his place John VIII. was elected. John grasped the reins of government firmly, and to the close of his life, kept the mutinous nobility sternly under.

During this Pope's reign the Saracens appeared again. They overran Southern Italy and threw the whole country into the wildest confusion. They marched upon Naples, Gaeta, Amalfi, Salerno, and forced the troops of the captured garrisons to fight in their own ranks. They then turned upon Rome, and with the co-operation of the fleet which was to attack the city from the sea, those terrible enemies of the Christian name resolved, once and for all, to raze the hated capital of Christendom to the ground. At this terrible moment when European society and Christianity itself seemed doomed, John VIII. was the only prince who prepared to resist the foe. The energy and activity he displayed on the occasion, may well put the other potentates of Europe to the blush. It was in vain he appealed to many of them for assistance. Those who did pretend to render any, were at best but slow and doubtful allies. Nay, this imminent danger to Rome and to Christendom was rather pleasing than otherwise to a few who fancied they saw therein some personal advantage to themselves.

The Saracens chose as a base of operations Vesuvius and Garagliano. They thus maintained their communications with Greece and Southern Italy, while they could advance at short notice upon the States of the Church. They only awaited now the arrival and co-operation of the numerous fleet which was to ascend the Tiber. The Pope hastily constructed a number of small vessels and equipped them as circumstances would best allow. He started in person for Naples to induce the duke to break off his sinful alliance with the Mahommedans. It was labor in vain. The alliance was advantageous to

Sergius and he would not renounce it. John placed him under the ban and hastened back to Rome. In his anxiety of mind he bethought him that St. Peter not only carried the keys but also the sword. Learning that the coasts of Fundi and Terracina were already wasted by the enemy, John hastened to Portus in person and immediately made sail with a number of small craft to meet the Mussulman. The two fleets sighted each other off Cape of Circe and closed in fight. Victory declared for the Papal galleys. John took eighteen of their ships, and set at liberty upwards of six hundred Christian slaves. Notwithstanding this splendid victory, John was unable to maintain his ground in Italy. He fled to France. But after a short stay he returned to Rome again. Of all the princes in Italy, there was not a single one, save himself, who could muster courage or resolution enough, to oppose the Saracens. Seeing that he was absolutely unable to maintain the unequal contest, John was at length driven to purchase immunity for his city and his states from the Infidel by the payment of a large tribute. His death, which took place in the year 882, relieved him from his heavy trials and labors. It is probable that he died a violent death at the hands of his personal enemies in the city. John VIII. was a man of a firm and determined, but withal, very equable character. His is the last of the great names in that glorious list of free and free-elected Roman Pontiffs of the ninth century. The political supremacy of the Popes was not, it must be owned, without its dangers and inconveniences. Nevertheless no argument of its nature could be more conclusive than is that drawn from the history of the sad seventy or eighty years after John's death, in favor of the necessity of such supremacy. Supreme political power is absolutely necessary to secure that independence of the Papacy, without which it is morally impossible for the Pope to govern the Church. The story of these years will make it evident to any thinking mind, that the Pope, to be free in religious matters, must, in temporals, be subject to no power whatsoever, be it king or kaiser, an aristocracy or democracy.

After John's demise, Rome and its environs became the prey of an ambitious faction of the nobility. The Holy See fell helplessly into their hands. The Church must now, in the person of her supreme head, drink the cup of shame to the dregs. That the Church outlived this dark period, is the paradox of history. It is a proof that God's own hand is with her and can deliver her when hope seems lost and all the powers of earth and hell are risen up to crush her. Now, from the annals of those dark days, we should learn a lesson for the present. History but repeats itself. We know what brought those evils beyond measure on the Church and such deep humiliation home to her children. The present is written in the past. Like causes will produce like effects again. And if there is any one truth inculcated more strongly than another in the whole course of centuries it is this,—that neither Romans nor Italians, neither King nor Kaiser nor President can do violence to the independence of the Holy See, without bringing certain destruction on themselves, and imperilling the peace of Europe. That indpendence is menaced in our day. European society and European civilization is therefore trembling on the brink of a precipice.

PART SECOND.

Jam ni te meritium Petri Pauliqus foveret,
Tempore jam longo Roma misella fores.

But for the aegis spread o'er thee by Peter and Paul,
Long since hadst thou, Rome, from the cities of earth disappeared.

I.
ROME WITHOUT PETER.

ROME without the Pope! As well conceive a bright day without the sun. Rome, and Rome no longer the city of the Apostles! Rome nothing but an every-day city of butchers and bakers, buyers and sellers, attorneys and druggists! Rome without the Holy Father! and who can picture to his mind or describe the city of nothingness, the city of ruin and desolation that would be left!

At the sight of any city that has lost its ancient splendor and importance, in whose streets and squares the grass shoots up, whose deserted storehouses and once gaudy palaces, now lie open to the four winds of heaven,—no matter what may have been the cause of the desolation, whether it was that the tide of commerce was turned from its gates, so that its merchants like those of Tyre and Sidon can no longer be the princes on 'change, or whether it was because the seat of empire was removed from its midst and the court transferred to a far-off city,— no matter what the reason, one cannot look on such a sight and not feel a dreariness of soul steal upon him corresponding to the dreary scene he gazes on. But were Rome once reduced to this condition what a picture of unutterable ruin she, that "city of dead empires" would present! Her condition would be worse than that of Athens where nothing more will flourish;—worse than Thebes, the granite quarry of the world, from which, for the last two thousand years, have been drawn those wonderful obelisks that stand scattered here and there in our modern cities, and which look in their loneliness as if they wept over the glories they had seen;—worse than Ninive or Persepolis, or Babylon with their mountains of brick and tile and vitrified rubbish;—in a word, Testaccio that hill of refuse and broken crockery outside her own gates, were the best representation of what Rome would be without the Pope. The Romans would be soon impoverished. The few that would remain, would be scattered through the city as the sparse inhabitants of a suburb. Their king would be the custodian of ill-kept museums, and their consuls, if they could retain even such officials, the antiquaries that would piece-meal sell Rome to the English. Such the condition to which the city would soon sink without the Holy Father.

Now are we drawing on our imagination for what we say. The page of history is open to all. It teaches us by what happened before, reasonably to infer what would happen under like circumstances again.

As we have already said, the Romans entered upon that high destiny to which their city was called, endowed with all those natural talents for which the Italians are so remarkable. They had the advantage, too, of an advanced degree of culture. They had the inspiring memories of their glorious past. But the old heathen spirit would at times break out in childish boasting, and in an unruly grasping at their chimerical idea of national power and greatness. It was with the Romans precisely as with a half-civilized barbarian. Old habits and vices will crop up from time to time in him, and for a season he will be the barbarian again. There was always a double Rome in history, or rather, as in the case of our barbarian, the old heathen principles were never thoroughly eradicated. From time to time as circumstances give them strength, these principles spring into action and often prevail for a period over the Christian idea. Rome regenerated, the Rome of the Popes, must then go under. Heathen principles triumph, and the city, for the time being, is heathen once more. The study of this perpetual conflict of the heathen and Christian principle in Rome, affords a lesson that he who runs may read. The Popes were never deprived of their authority in Rome, were never compelled to take refuge elsewhere, that the city was not in consequence reduced to poverty and desolation, that Rome did not become a meaningless nothing among the cities of the earth.

The darkest days of Roman history are those in which she was alas too truly SECULARIZED in the hands of petty tyrants and wanton debauchees. At that same period Christianity in other lands was giving birth to the noblest institutions. It produced numerous eminent and holy men whose learning was as profound as their piety was sincere. And while the Church thus flourished and was honored in her children, the Romans were learning in the blood that stained their streets and the debaucheries that polluted their homes, what Rome would be without the Pope, or what was just as bad, what she would be with a Pope not free or one not freely elected. These were seventy years with very few glimmerings of light indeed to relieve the dismal cast of the picture. To this period of the degradation of the Papacy, to those years of trouble and complete confusion of all social and moral rights, succeeded another sad period in the history of the Church. The Popes were arbitrarily set up by the German Kaiser, and though, as far as the Ottos at least were concerned, some regard was had to merit, the principle was ruinous, as it destroyed the freedom of the Church and subjected the spiritual power almost completely to the will of the emperor.

Then followed the other seventy years of exile at Avignon. Here mid the most trying vexations, the Popes frequently deprived of their natural counsellors had to perform their weighty duties to the Church and solve the most intricate questions on all manner of subjects. They were not always free as to the decisions to be given, and even when they were so, the evil was almost as great, for the world did not think them free. What, let us ask, was Rome during these seventy years? We shall answer further on. In passing, we may remark that the States of the Church were dismembered, and that anarchy and the dagger ruled in Rome. The few pilgrims who then visited the tomb of the Apostles appeared, as the eminent Villani expressed it, "like sheep among a parcel of wolves." Then burst the terrible revolution at the end of the last century over Europe, a revolution which we have seen feebly echoed in our own times. Pius VI., Pius VII. and Pius IX. were taken prisoners at Rome or forced to fly the city. What was Rome during their absence?

In the following pages we shall endeavor to throw some light on these important periods of Roman history, and show where the proper place and real interests of Rome lie.

II.

SECULARIZED ROME OF THE NINTH CENTURY.

The Popes, as we have already remarked, acquired a glorious place in European history during the middle ages. That place, unfortunately for European society and civilization, they were not destined long to hold. Charlemagne was crowned at Rome in the year 800. Before the close of the ninth century, the great monarchy which he had so laboriously built up, had melted into nothing. Internal dissensions and civil wars had gnawed away its vitals, and the constant division and subdivision of the territory into independent principalities completed the dissolution. Nor was there, when the Frankish empire thus dwindled away, any other strong power that could wield a steadying influence in European affairs. The Church was deprived of her advowee, and the Pope, devoid of any competent armed force, was unable to prevent ambitious neighbors from seizing on portions of his states. The doings of the nobility in the city itself were still more deplorable. They took the election of the Popes into their own hands, and only men who were ready to devote themselves unconditionally to the faction or family interests of their patrons, could hope to be admitted to the chair of St. Peter.

Through their extensive family connections and alliances, some of the Romans at that time were possessed of great power and influence. The Kaiser gone, they had no one to fear. Among them were found some very bad men. These gave themselves up in the most unblushing manner to every species of vice. They feared neither God nor man, and when there was a point to gain or a passion to be gratified, stopped at no crime however enormous. The Pope is either their prisoner in a dungeon, or a fugitive from the city, to escape their violence, or a man, as it sometimes happened, of their own stamp and party. The Christian world had to look on and see the Papacy dishonored and abused by a faction of violent and godless Roman nobles. They had as little respect for the city and the Roman name, as they had for the outraged Apostolic dignity. Some of these wretches, Gregory and his son-in-law George, with others equally infamous, actually plundered the Lateran basilica and other churches, and this while the Saracens were in the neighborhood wasting the Campagna with fire and sword. The robbers made away out of the city at night with their sacrilegious booty, leaving one of the gates of Rome wide open. Had even some one family or faction been strong enough not only to seize the reins of power but also to hold them, things had never come to such a woeful condition. But it was now one faction and then another held sway. The Romans of these days, it would seem, used all their might to annihilate the Papacy. Its possessions—the "Patrimony"—was the booty of a thousand robbers. Ten times within a few years was the city on the point of being demolished. The cities, towns and villages all round were pulled down, their inhabitants stripped or murdered and their bishops put to flight. All who could escape took shelter within the walls of Rome. In the adjoining towns and rural districts, not a soul remained, man, woman or child. A strange and dense darkness overspread the city. The dark forms of the furious and factious barons of the city and Campagna, might be seen rushing through the fog, fighting with, and murdering each other, burning and destroying all before them. At length from this fermenting chaos of wild licentiousness rose by degrees, certain families and certain individuals above their fellows, until finally one of them was able to declare himself dictator.

Within eight years, no less than eight Popes were set up and hurled down. The streets of Rome were running with the blood of her citizens. Faction met faction in fierce fray, and the dagger was in constant service. The government of the city passed into the hands of laics, the *"judices de militia"* as they called themselves.

We may well say of those years that fiction cannot fancy anything equal to fact. The barons of Spoletto,—the so-called national party,—had intruded one of their own faction into the Apostolic chair. The blind fanatacism of party hate not unfrequently disturbed the repose of the dead. A long deceased predecessor of the new Pope must now be solemnly deposed and excommunicated. A synod was assembled for the purpose in February or March

897. The corpse which had been over eight months in the grave was exhumed. Clad in its pontifical robes, it was brought in its putrifying condition from the tomb of St. Peter's to the council-hall. While the body emitted its putrid stench through the hall, the prosecutor arose, and with juridical solemnity put the question:—"Why hast thou ambitiously usurped the Apostolic Chair?" The dead man was condemned, the robes torn from the corpse, three fingers of the right hand were cut off, and then mid the jeers of the rabble and the most barbarous shouting the decaying body was wildly dragged from the hall along the streets and cast into the Tiber. As the inhuman drama closed, the Lateran basilica in which the synod of deposition had been held, fell with a crash to the earth. Stephen VI. who was induced by his relatives to go through that revolting farce, suffered the most mortal agonies in the neighboring palace in which he dwelt. Stephen himself was subsequently strangled in prison. After his death, the body of Formosus was picked up by fishermen and brought back to its tomb. The horrified Romans relate that the pictures and statues of the chapel bowed their heads in reverence as the unhappy dead was brought in.

Such was the horrible condition of things in "secularized" Rome:—utter contempt of all law human and divine, fierce hate and savage revenge, lust unbridled, wild ambition, and the maddest intoxication of human reason. History itself is silent in the wild commotion. The only records of this fearful period that have reached us are found in the acts of some two synods. John IX. became Pope. His reign was too brief to allow him to undo the scandalous acts of his predecessors. His earliest attention was given to the synod that sat in judgment on the corpse. He assembled his council. All the bishops and priests who had signed the decision were cited. They pleaded that they were forced to do so by the lawless barons. They cast themselves upon their knees before the Pope and sued for pardon. The synod was formally condemned. Those who had taken a guilty part in it were placed under the ban, and the faction that had profaned the sanctity of the grave had to fly the city, to escape the indignant burst of popular feeling which their sacrilegious conduct now called forth. They fled to Tuscany, but only bided their opportunity to enter Rome again. Surely, this was a horrible state of affairs. But we have not yet stated the worst. The condition of the whole country was as bad as that of Rome. "Small choice," says the proverb, "in rotten apples," and it were indeed hard to choose between the bloody and reckless factions that desolated Rome, the hordes of fierce Magyars that wasted the North, and the Saracens in the South, who from their stronghold of Garagliano devastated the country for miles around, for the space of thirty years. Such, SECULARIZED Rome, such, Italy in those times.

There was only one man then, who took the honor of Rome and the Italian name to heart, and that one man was a Pope, John X. Just because he did so however, he was vilified on all sides, and made the butt of every calumny that the wretched party-spirit of the times could devise. It was only in recent times, after history was written anew, that the name of John X. was at length extricated from the pile of calumny heaped upon it, and presented to the world as that of a man who was great enough to rise above the grovelling influences of his day and do honor to Rome, when she was steeped in dishonor by her lay rulers.

III.
ROME UNDER THE TYRANNICAL DYNASTIES OF THE TENTH CENTURY.

THAT the Papacy and the Papacy alone was all these years the only hope for Italy even in a political point of view, is abundantly proved by the fact, that, whenever the Holy See regained even a little of its freedom, Italy looked up and gave promise of better things even if she did not always produce them. Enslave the Pope and the country goes to ruin. But too few, alas! and far between, were the intervals of freedom enjoyed during this period by the Popes.

The hundred-headed hydra of faction rose again. John X., who vanquished the Saracens at Garagliano, was no match for this monster. Rome is again hidden in darkness, and Italy a prey to the most frightful anarchy. The lewd Marozia ruled the city. She set her bastard son in the chair of St. Peter. The voice of history is hushed upon the affairs of Rome during his reign. During the sway of his mother and her party, the city is sunk in darkness, and things were as bad or worse, if possible, throughout the rest of Italy.

It was the year 930. Hugo in the North of Italy declared himself king. He was an intriguing, crafty man, licentious and ambitious. He was as bold and daring to conceive, as he was unscrupulous and prompt to carry out his plans of aggrandizement. His ambition was to establish himself king of all Italy, and be crowned at Rome on the Capitol. Marozia herself invited and pressed him to enter Rome. The government of the city was, in reality, no longer in the hands of the Pope. Hugo came, but was soon after driven in disgrace from the city by Alberich, another natural son of that ill-famed woman. Alberich now snatched the reigns of power out of his mother's hands, and formally introduced into Rome the system of the tyrants of the ancient cities of Greece. The Romans had to recognize him as their lord. He styled himself "Alberich, Prince and Senator of all the Romans." Rome now tried to descend from the rank of capital of Christendom, and take place by the side of the little Italian duchies and principalities of Benevento, Naples, Tuscany, Venice, etc.

The power of Alberich rested on his wide and influential family connections, on his immense wealth, and his popularity with the Roman aristocracy. This bold man acted the absolute king of Rome for a considerable time. In all his public acts and documents, however, the name of the Pope and the year of his reign were mentioned as if the latter really reigned. History does not accuse Alberich of the crimes committed by his cotemporaries. He seems to have been a man of firm character, and to have wielded his power with a strong and steady hand. He held the weak Popes whose names he made use of completely under his dominion. He set them up at will, and pulled them down in like manner, as in the case of Stephen VIII., if they hesitated to become the willing tools of his policy. They were generally however very pliable, for Alberich was careful in his choice. It is written for instance of Marinus II. "that he in all things obeyed the commands of his prince, without whose orders the good man attempted nothing." *Electus Marinus Papa non audebat adtingere aliquid extra jussionem Alberici principis.*

Under such circumstances the Popes, not unfrequently, could neither act the part of the vigilant bishop nor that of the honest man. Alberich's policy occasionally demanded acts on their part which such characters could not perform. Alberich died in the year 954. But the "Prince of Rome" had learned before his death, that the separation of the spiritual from the temporal power in the city of St. Peter could not be of lasting duration. He accordingly assembled the Roman nobles in St. Peter's, a short time before he died, and had them solemnly to swear that his son and heir, Octavian should be elected Pope. Pursuant to this oath, the boy who could have hardly reached his sixteenth year, and already displayed every indication of early profligacy, was actually thrust into the Apostolic chair. In the person of this grand-son of Marozia, the Papacy was reduced to its deepest degradation, and Rome to the lowest depth of dishonor and humiliation.

Rome is now fully SECULARIZED. She is become the capital of an obscure and petty duchy. The Pope and the Papacy are at the mercy of her petty rulers. That sublime power which was raised up by

God to preside over Christendom, is wielded at will by a despicable tyrant. Rome's own high calling is lost sight of. The light of science, even ecclesiastical science, burned never so faintly. It seemed on the point of being extinguished altogether. But we know the causes of this dark desolation. No need to be surprised at the results. Such results from such causes are as natural as they are invariable. People in other lands were at that time completely bewildered. They could not understand what they witnessed. In a synod held at Rheims, the bishops said to the Papal legates:—"At the present day in Rome there is scarcely a single man who knows enough to be ordained ostiarius. With what face then can those at Rome undertake to teach us and the world what they know nothing about themselves? Such gross ignorance is unpardonable in the bishop of Rome, whose duty it is to decide on matters of faith, moral and, discipline throughout the whole Church."

The Patrimony of St. Peter, the Papal States, which had been acquired to the Church by the patient industry of centuries, all now fell into the hands of different lay lords. Rome and its immediate vicinity nominally remained to the Church. But, as we have seen, it was SECULARIZED to the full. The Crescentii seized on the Sabine territory and Præneste; the duke of Tuscany occupied Southern Tuscany together with the duchies of Spoleto and Camerino. Ravenna with its surrounding district and the Pentapolis were likewise lost to the Holy See. The only source of income left the Popes, were a few fiefs that had escaped the general spoliation. All the treasures of the Church were squandered—squandered with a prodigality scandalous even for those days of scandal. In after time, everything had to be purchased anew. It took more than two centuries to heal the wounds which that SECULARIZATION inflicted on the Church. The city of Rome was as severe a sufferer, and the dishonor which the Romans of those days brought upon themselves and the Roman name, remains, to Rome's eternal disgrace, indelibly written on the page of history.

IV.

NOMINATION OF THE POPES BY THE GER- MAN KAISER.

By the unworthy manner in which they had begun to dispose of the Holy See, the Roman nobility had brought disgrace upon all Christendom. Their example was afterwards followed by the German emperors; first, by those of the house of Saxony, afterwards, by those of the Frankish dynasty. This lasted for about a period of ninety years, say in round numbers, from 960 to 1050.

After such a night of dreary darkness, it is really refreshing to see towards the close of the tenth century, in the year 996, two vigorous and noble spirits at once arise, the one at the head of the spiritual power of Christendom, the other, master of the temporal. These were the German Pope Gregory V. and the German emperor Otto III. The young Pope scarcely five and twenty years of age, was as learned as he was truly pious. Otto was called the prodigy (*Weltwunder*) of his time. These twin spirits were the Christian Castor and Pollux of that age, and the dawn of the glorious morrow promised by their reign, lit up the closing days of that darkest of dark ages, the tenth century. With such a Pope and such an emperor united as they were by the ties of blood as well as by kindred feelings and sentiments, it was hopefully believed that that era which the best and purest souls in Christendom had long been praying for, was at last inaugurated. Church and State seemed to repose on that foundation which is safest for both,—close harmony and unanimity between their supreme rulers.

But Gregory's reign was short. Still the shade cast upon the glorious prospect by his death was not of long duration. A worthy successor to Gregory, the venerable Archbishop Gerbert, under the name of Sylvester II., was soon raised to the Apostolic chair. Gerbert had seen much of the world. He had been tutor to the young emperor, and had formerly been a Benedictine abbot. He was considered the most accomplished scholar of his age. Pope and Kaiser are again in harmonious union, and, as the tenth century closed, the most cordial understanding existed between the two.

But neither Gregory nor Sylvester was freely elected. They were appointed directly by Otto III. as their immediate predecessors were by Otto the Great and Otto II. With the Christian view of rescuing the Papacy from the disgraceful Roman factions, the emperors took upon themselves to name the Pope. Experience had not yet taught them that nothing whatever can be so ruinous to the Church as the want of freedom especially in the choice of her supreme head, the Pope.

All three of the Ottos, father, son and grandson, came to look upon the Holy See as a benefice at their disposal. It was viewed as an appendage to the imperial power. Otto the Great from the moment of his coronation charged himself with the advowson of the Church. But the manner of his protection was that of a formal wardship. It really amounted to a complete subjection of the Holy See to himself. With a high hand he set aside John XII., that son of Alberich, and appointed another in his stead. John was not a worthy Pope, but he was nevertheless the lawfully elected one. Otto assumed exclusive control of the Pontifical elections. The canonical ones held, were mere farces. The voters had simply to ratify Otto's nomination. Nor did he ground his interference on the actual necessities of the times, seeing what a state of things existed in Rome. No, he claimed the right of placing whom he would in the Papal chair, and looked upon this right, as we said before, as a natural appendage of the imperial power. Against any such assumption of power on the part of the temporal ruler, the whole history of the Church protested. There was no precedent for it, save what the late bloody factions of the Roman nobility afforded. The latter would in all likelihood have continued to exercise such power over the Papacy still, had not Otto resolved to have a voice too in such an important matter. And Otto had the means of making his voice heard and his word prevail. In his new pretensions, he was merely substituting his command in this regard, for that of some Roman faction. There is no denying, that with Otto, the Holy See fared better than it did, or ever would, fare at the hands of the reckless Roman nobility. These were devoid of all principle. They sought only their own interests. Nevertheless, Otto's principle was pregnant with more dangerous consequences to the Church than were the vile factions of Rome. Very probably the Kaiser had the Byzantine empire in his mind at the time, and believed that he, as emperor of the West, ought to be there allowed to exercise the same control over ecclesiastical matters, that the emperor of the East exercised throughout his dominions.

It was necessary for Otto's plans, that the head of the Church should enter into, and further, his great political views. Besides he was master of Italy. He had caried off the Subalpine monarch Berengarius prisoner and deposed John XII. To counteract the aversion of the Romans to the Germans, he wanted a Pope who would favor his own Germanizing policy. He should have one who would understand the imperial interests as they were understood by himself. Still it must be regarded as a great step in the right direction that the Papacy was extricated from the Roman factions. Worthy and competent men could be, and were now elected. In a word, Otto extorted from the Romans complete submission in all things to the imperial rule. They had not only to forego all voice in the election of the Pontiff but had also to swear allegiance to Otto's government. As long as the German power in Italy lasted, they were compelled to do the same by each of his successors. But a wrong—a most pernicious principle was involved in the Kaiser's pretensions. No man, no power on earth can be admitted to hold the exclusive right of nominating to the See of Peter.

The attempt to enforce that principle failed. Like all other attempts of the kind it defeated itself. The principle has been tried at the bar of history, and a verdict against it returned. It could not pass. It was acted on for the last time in 1050 by the emperor Henry III. From that time on, the spirit of ecclesiastical independence began to wax stronger, and both powers—the spiritual and the temporal—entered each upon a new path more befitting their respective aims and attributes.

V.

ITALIAN NATIONALITY.

LET us now turn our thoughts a moment from these heart-sickening reflections on the condition of the "Eternal City," to some considerations of a more general character.

Different nations as different individuals have their own endowments. One has this, another that. The man who would learn anything from history beyond bare names, and dates, and square miles, should not fail to take into account the peculiar characteristics of each people. By so doing, he will discover that the interests of one nation are not necessarily those of another, and that events in one country, are frequently to be regarded in a different light from what similar events should be in another. He will find, too, that a nation's best interests are consulted, when its political form or institutions are allowed to grow up and develop themselves in accordance with the genius and characteristics of the people, not when the people are violently forced to accept this or that idea. We have no hesitation in saying that Italy, like Switzerland, is a land that can never thrive under one general government. Nay, of the two, we should say that the attempt to bring the Swiss under one rule would be more successful than it would be with the Italians. The different parts of Italy are as different as can be from each other. They are different in appearance, in climate, in products. Italy along the coasts is nothing like the Italy of the interior. Again, the inhabitants of the different provinces of this country naturally so diversified, are, and have been, since the twilight of history as unlike each other as the soils they dwell on. It was so before the rise of Rome, it continued so during the Republic, and was left so when the empire passed away. The successive invasions from the North, left behind a great many of the German elements on Italian soil. Many of the Northern tribes only swept like a hurricane over the land, but settlements more or less permanent were made by the Heruli, the Ostrogoths, the Lombards, the Saracens, and the Franco-Normans. Hence arose an admixture of several different peoples, and for a considerable time the foreign element was the more prevailing. In whole districts sometimes, nothing but German, or Greek, or Arabic, was spoken. This admixture did not take place, or at least, only to a very small extent in Rome itself, or in the States of the Church. It was from this reservoir that the Italian element spread again and finally absorbed all others. The foreign tongues grew obsolete by degrees, and laws, moulded after the Roman code, were substituted for the more imperfect and confused jurisprudence of the foreign settlements. The character of the Italians is naturally what might be expected from such a state of things. Individuality is there much more easily developed than elsewhere, and is entitled to far higher consideration. An Italian of the most ordinary condition of life, feels that he is free from want. The little that he needs is supplied, and abundantly supplied, by the generous soil. In ease and leisure he cultivates his tastes and improves his mind. That gross ignorance to which an over-measure of manual and bodily labor dooms so many of the people in Germany, France and England, is not met with in Italy. The Italian, taken in himself, is really a respectable individual. Man for man, you would go through a thousand of his class in Northern Europe, be they laborers, tradesmen, scholars or soldiers, before you would find one so well qualified to enjoy and to appreciate the pleasures of the mind and the imagination, or move and dress with such an air of grace and easy dignity as appears natural to the Italian. Nevertheless, though strange, if you will, it is incontestable, that in Italy, where the intellectual and physical development of the individual is so superior, the body-politic wears the contrary aspect. The polished, ease-loving Italian could develop only the municipal system of government. It is the only one that bears on his own every day life and habits. It is on this account, that in very small states of Italy which grew up in accordance with the natural bent of the local inhabitants, whether into a monarchial or republican form of government, we not unfrequently find, art and social refinement to have reached the very highest degree of perfection. But we have never seen, and never shall see, any large, compact, uniform state arise in the country. The artful and violent measures now taken to create such a state, are as foreign and unnatural to the Italian turn of mind as they are novel in Italian history.

With such manifold differences of soil and people, it may seem strange to speak of the Italian nation or Italian nationality. Nevertheless, there always was, and still is such a thing. That nationality is sharply defined, too, and possesses characteristics which other less gifted nations may well envy. Let us only take care not to look for this nationality in the wrong place. To understand, if not even to recognize it, we should ourselves have a taste for intellectual grandeur and the beautiful in art. We should also learn to appreciate Italian genius taken in itself, even when in other respects it is saddled with many defects and infirmities. The populace of that whole country from Venice to Naples in which the beautiful in art is studied and admired, and the amenities of social life are so highly cultivated, forms one grand intellectual nationality. This is the genuine and only real Italian nationality that exists now, or ever did exist. The groundwork of this glorious nationality was the full and free development of the different parts of the country according to their local tastes and habits. Had Mantua, Venice, Milan, Ferrara, Alessandria, Genoa, Pisa, Lucca, Sienna, Florence or Naples been never more than little, provincial towns of an extensive, centralized Italian kingdom, modern history would have little reason to dwell on them with pleasure as lights of science and literature. But fortunately for themselves and the world, each one of these cities was once a free and independent republic. Then, too, was each of them the centre of a flourishing trade and wide commerce, and the industry of the citizens only kept pace with their progress in the fine arts and all manner of intellectual attainments. In these little states, the highest political principles were evolved and applied in practice, while the larger kingdoms of the period had hardly yet learned the elements of political science. Each city was a sovereign power, *sui juris*, and lived its own peculiar life. Thus was engendered in the citizens that strong love of freedom. They were ready to defend their rights and liberties against all and every opponent. They resisted the powerful and high-handed Kaiser Barbarossa, to the last, and, in revenge, Frederic at the point of the sword, made these little Italian republics sorely feel the weight of his imperial power.

The political unity which fortunately for herself, Italy did not possess at that time, was richly compensated for by her religious unity. Many a time, her spiritual chief was found at the head of a combination of these little allies, in support of Italian independence. The Pope headed the Lombard alliance against Frederic. He opposed might and main the short-sighted despotism of Barbarossa, who would fain level and amalgamate all things to suit his own narrow views, and thereby destroy the noble and rich peculiarities of these little, independent communities. In this genuine Italian effort, as in defence of every national right and liberty of the country, the Popes invariably led the way for the many other eminent patriots. And so is it, even to this day. For, surely Pius IX. leaving all else aside, is a better, a truer Italian (pardon the comparison) than that half-barbarian who calls himself king of Italy. One should certainly have very little brains to allow himself to be misled by the affected patriotism of our days. He must be very ignorant on the subject of European history, who can fail to recognize the proper sphere of the Italians, and what it is that conduces to the greatness and glory of Italy. And, reading the lesson of the past, none but a narrow-minded bigot or a man of perverted conscience, could deny that the Popes are the proper, the only persons to extend that sphere, and be the guardians of the real, the genuine nationality of Italy. And so we see in that small portion of this lovely land—the States of the Church—that the different provinces were united and strong in the Popes, and, through the Popes, they were free. The provinces with their municipal rights, enjoyed the utmost freedom. Indeed, in some cases, it amounted to almost complete independence. Let those who revile the Papal government, look into the Roman municipal regulations of 1850. Either these men talk of what they know not, or there is not a particle of principle or of honor left them. A German, or Frenchman, who even in his very house is subject to an annoying government interference, may pride himself indeed that he has a voice in the politics of the nation. A genuine Italian would think such empty bauble a very poor indemnity for the loss of his municipal importance and freedom. The peculiarities of his character require the most perfect liberty of action as to all that lies immediately around him. The new-fangled kingdom of Italy is not yet quite centralized. It never will be, it never can be, until it has stamped out the national character,—this genuine Italian nationality. This unity without uniformity is factitious. It is un-Italian. It wont work. The different Italian castes can never be forced under one ruler and one system. Notwithstanding, the political fever with which they now burn, the Italians love their personal and municipal liberties. They cling to their traditional customs and peculiarities. These are much dearer to the individual, than national unity. An alliance between the several Italian states might serve all interests: unity will not. The imposts of blood and treasure which they are called on to meet, will soon give the Italians enough of their new unity, to say nothing of the huge swindle going on in the new capital of Italy.

The Romans, in whom the national characteristics are most deeply impressed, have, at times, given excessive way to their passion for individual and communal liberty. Sometimes, too, they violently strove to carry out their principles throughout the whole of the Papal States. Not unfrequently were these movements set down to revolutionary credit and dissatisfaction with the government by those who hate and oppose, on all occasions, the sacred ruler of City and States.

VI.

THE VATICAN AND THE CAPITOL.

The unlimited moral power which Rome, even in the melancholy times, still exercised over the young nations of Europe, shows itself in many touching examples. Canute, the Danish king and conqueror of England, went on a pilgrimage to Rome. It was during the reign of Conrad II. The city was at the time the theatre of the wild brawls and bloody encounters of the factious Roman nobility. They quarrelled among themselves, and quarrelled unceasingly with the rough Germans who were now in Rome. In a beautiful letter which has reached our time, Canute writing from Rome to the English people, speaks of the happiness it gave him to venerate all the shrines and relics of the city. He tells them how he had prayed God to grant him wisdom to govern henceforth well, that the sins and short-comings of his youth may be expiated by the piety of his declining years. Such the impression the "Eternal City" made on foreigners, even in those days, when the Romans themselves were, alas, so far removed from that ideal height to which they were called in virtue of their historical relation to Christianity.

But, henceforward we are never again to see a faction Pope or an imperial one occupying the Holy

Chair. The freedom of the Papal elections is established. The choice for the future is to be exclusively, as well as conclusively, made by the illustrious college of Cardinals. The history of the city, however, and that of St. Peter's successor, separate wider from each other, than ever they were before. The Papacy came to be more and more recognized as the tribunal of Europe. The narrow municipal spirit of the Romans, on the contrary, was every day growing more petty and less capable of comprehending the intellectual and moral superiority to which their city, as the see of St. Peter, was called. From this time forward, we see the Romans becoming perfectly demented on the subject of old memories and glories. The S. P. Q. R. Senate and People of Rome appear in all the official documents of the city. Rome, with her senate, what would she be? Nothing more than an obscure provincial city. Yet the Romans were so senseless and crazy on the idea, that the ablest Popes, as Gregory VII. and Innocent III., were forced to seek temporary shelter elsewhere.

As sovereign of Rome and the States of the Church, the Pope's political independence was theoretically secured. But for a long time, his tenure of these states was anything but secure. The Kaiser was the Papal advowee. His protection was often rather injurious and damaging to the Church than otherwise. On that ground, he sought to meddle in all matters and frequently obstructed the action of the Popes. It took centuries of strife and toil, ere the complete independence of the Pope was established. This was not until it was guaranteed by the European powers and recognized in the law of nations.

The Papal rule was so very, very mild in his States, that the several little cities scarcely felt it at all. They enjoyed almost absolute independence. At Rome, the lay lords filled all the government offices. Though the Pope or his representative was chief of the administration, this seemed often only a nominal thing. Since the right of choosing the Pope, which had been so long and so disgracefully abused, was taken altogether out of the hands of the nobility, they held most tenaciously to the right of choosing their own city officials. The olden glories of Rome are trumped up oftener than ever. The titles of senator, consul, pro-consul, and the like, appear in the official lists. When a Roman was appointed governor of a little department or neighboring town, he is "Pro-consul." In Rome, we have the *"Patres Conscripti."* The assemblies of the nobles which were held in an ancient circus or hippodrome were called, "Sessions of the Senate." The fever about the olden Republic grew hotter and hotter, 'till at length it led to the proclamation of that fantastic republic of which we shall presently speak.

The Popes at this period took up their permanent abode in the Vatican. On this site Eugenius III., Celestin III., Innocent III., and Nicholas III., had erected magnificent palaces and laid out splendid gardens. But the Popes were frequently driven from their homes by the republicanizing Romans, and wandered, homeless fugitives, from one town to another, while the Christian world listened with reverence and attention to the words that fell from their lips. They generally found shelter in one or other of the towns of the Papal States, Anagni, Viterbo or Rieti. But there were times when they were obliged to betake themselves to a foreign territory altogether, till the storm had blown over. It was then said of the Pope: *Pulsus ab Urbe, ab Orbe recipitur,*—"driven from the city, he is welcomed by the world." It went so far that a formal war was sometimes waged between the "Romans" and the "Papists" or Papal party. This happened in 1235. The Romans were defeated before Viterbo. Hostilities continued, however, and an edict was issued declaring that the Pope was forever banished from Rome unless he came to their terms.

Conditions of peace were at length mutually agreed upon. The document in which they were drawn up, will give us a good idea of the city government. We transcribe the following:—"We, by the grace of God, noble citizens of the illustrious City, promise as the plenipotentiaries of the illustrious senate, and by command, and with, the approbation of the renowed Roman commons who assembled on the Capitol at the sound of bells and trumpets, ... that we, in obedience to the Pope's orders, are willing to make reparation .... that we withdraw, on the authority of the Senate and the people, the acts of proscription and the edicts that have been issued. Further, to remove all cause of dissension between us and the Church and the Pope, whom, through reverence for Christ, Whose vicar he is, and the Prince of the Apostles, whose successor he is, we respect as pious children, as also, because it is conducive to the honor of this illustrious and renowned City, we hereby deree: that ecclesiastical persons in, or outside Rome, or the families of the Popes and Cardinals, shall not be brought before the civil courts nor shall they be driven thereto by the undermining of their houses, nor in any other way.... We give eternal peace to the Emperor and to his vassals, the citizens of Anagni, Viterbo, Velletri, Segni.... and to all others of the Patrimony, and all friends of the Church, etc."

Sometimes the Popes remained a considerable time out of Rome. They grew sick of dealing with the rebellious citizens. On such occasions, the Romans were sure to wish him back. Threats and entreaties would be used to induce him to return. The Romans would then argue:—the Pope is not bishop of Anagni, or Perugia, or Lyons, but of Rome. They, at one time, threatened to make war upon the inhabitants of Perugia, if they would not compel the Pope, who had taken refuge with them, to return to Rome. This happened under Innocent IV. Nicholas III. was a man of steel. He held Rome well under, and ruled with a firm hand. Nicholas' predecessors, even under the most adverse circumstances, were always the boldest and most persevering advocates of national independence. They resisted to the last, the powerful Hohenstaufen emperors. Gregory IX. manfully held out against that inveterate foe of all civil liberty or municipal independence, Frederic II. Once Frederic with a large army lay before the walls of Rome. Some parties who were within the walls, but devoted to the imperial interests, cried out:—"The kaiser, the kaiser is there himself, we must give up the city." Gregory heard it. He ordered a solemn procession with the relics of the Holy Cross, and the heads of the Apostles Peter and Paul. Arrived at St. Peter's, the relics were deposited on the high altar. The Pope lifted the tiara from his head, and laid it on the relics. He then turned to the people and said: "Your Saints will defend this Rome which you Romans are ready to sacrifice." The traitors were gained over. The kaiser who counted on co-operation from within failed to take the city. He had to withdraw towards Apulia. In a letter to the Romans from this place, he manifests his chagrin. "It pains us," he writes in the old bombastic style, "that of the many thousands of the old stock of Romulus, both nobles and quirites, not a single man was found courageous enough to declare for us." This choice defender of the Church then goes on to urge the Romans, under pain of incurring his highest displeasure, to revolt against the Pope.

The Senate-Chamber, the seat of the Republic, stood on the Capitol near the Tarpean rock. There the senators assembled. The city council held their sessions in a neighboring and much better looking building, a Franciscan monastery, erected on the site of the ancient palace of Octavian. This Roman senate-chamber had nothing to recommend it, save its big name, and the circumstance that it stood on the ruins of noble reminiscences. It was a half-ancient, half-modern structure that seemed as much out of place, as the senators who occupied it. These pigmy officials dated their little city ordinances from the Capitol, while decrees for the government of the world were issued from the neighboring Vatican. And such were the Lilluputian republicans who more than once rose in arms against the spiritual lord of Christendom.

VII.
THE POPES AT AVIGNON.

THE elevation of the house of Anjou to the throne of Sicily, was an important event in the history of Rome and the Papacy. Two brothers could scarcely be more unlike than St. Louis of France, and his brother, Charles of Anjou. When the Pope had to make choice of a sovereign for the vacant throne of Sicily, Charles was the man selected. It is one of the most extraordinary phenomena of history, that the Popes who can never be deceived in deciding on questions of faith or morals, should sometimes seem to be the easiest of dupes in other matters. In Charles, the Pope reposed the most unbounded confidence. Yet by him were the temporal possessions of the Church brought into the greatest jeopardy, and almost entirely lost. It was the grossest blunder on the part of the Pope to confer the crown of Sicily, on such an unprincipled and ambitious prince. True, France had in former times done more for the independence of the Papacy than any other nation of Christendom. Therefore we need not wonder that the Pope, finding in the Kaiser but a sorry reed to lean upon, turned to the house of Capet. Besides, at the very period in question, the house of Capet could well pride itself on the virtues of the saintly Crusader. Accordingly, when the crown of Naples was forfeited by its German possessor for the crime of treason, it was conferred on the French prince, Charles of Anjou. But no sooner was Anjou named king of Naples, than French influence in all Roman affairs was felt to be omnipotent. French Popes were elected, French cardinals were created, and Popes and cardinals did all they could to further French influence in ecclesiastico-political matters. Frenchmen were appointed governors of provinces throughout the Papal States. Martin IV., a Frenchman, created Charles a Roman senator. And now this Franco-Roman senator assumed the performance of the civil functions of the Pope who no longer resided in Rome. The relations of the Pope with the inhabitants of his states were broken off. The Papacy after a while became the exclusive property of the French nation. To these French Popes, Italy was a foreign country. They preferred to dwell on their own soil. The removal of the Papal court altogether to Avignon was the consequence. Here it remained for the space of seventy years. At Avignon, a new and a fearful trial awaited the Papacy. The Popes were, or at least seemed to be, held prisoners in the hands of St. Louis' grandson. The circumstances which first drove the Popes into France, might perhaps be traced to the hostility of the German emperors. But the residence at Avignon entailed unquestionably far greater evils on the Church than all the molestations of the Kaiser.

The States of the Church now lost all their significance. They were considered at Avignon and dealt with merely as a distant province deserving of no great attention and to be managed by a vice-gerent. As to the far-off city of Rome, in which the Popes, while they clung to it, could never feel free, the French resident at Avignon troubled himself very little.

In the year 1300, was written one bright and glorious page of Roman story. It was just before the removal of the Papal court to Avignon. Pope Boniface VIII. announced the great centenary jubilee. Countless throngs of pilgrims (the Romans say two millions) visited the Holy City that year. Day after day, Rome saw a new crowd arrive. The Campagna, as well as the city itself, resounded with the hymns and sacred songs of the pilgrims. They spoke in many different tongues, but they sang their hymns and psalms in the common language of the Church. The ardent longings of all those pilgrims from many lands, were directed to the self-same spot, and, as the sun-lit view of that forest of spires in the "Eternal City" broke upon their sight in the distance, they would cry out in exultation, "*Roma! Roma!*" like sailors at sight of land, after a weary voyage. At the gates, they were received by persons employed for the purpose and conducted to their respective inns, or, as was more generally the case, taken first all together to St. Peter's to pray at the tomb of the Apostles.

Those pilgrims having satisfied their devotional feelings turned their astonished gaze on the monuments of the city. In this classical spot, lived the noblest reminiscences of antiquity. Here, too, stood the noblest monuments of Christianity. These monuments majestically proclaimed the high destiny of Rome, of which they were themselves at once the proof and the expression. All these pilgrims assembled in the world's great temple of the New Dispensation. The august mysteries of the redemption were celebrated before them. It was the jubilee year of the New Covenant. The strangers saw the successor of St. Peter in all his sublime majesty. They knelt in reverential awe to receive the solemn blessing which was given by Christ's vice-gerent on earth to the City and to the world from the Loggie which Pope Boniface had erected expressly for the occasion.

The jubilee closed on Christmas night 1300. The Pope announced the closing, and again gave his benediction to the home-returning pilgrims. This year, 1300, is a great epoch in the history of Rome and the Papacy. This year of joy and festivity was soon followed by sorrows. Boniface underwent his tragical sufferings and death; his successors were in exile at Avignon; and the city saw a long and cheerless day of desolation and desertion.

VIII.
THE GHOST OF ANCIENT PAGANISM IN THE RUINS OF ROME.

WHEN the Papal Court was transferred to Avignon, Rome appeared like a corpse from which the vital breath had departed. For a short while indeed the body still retains the appearance of life, but it soon falls into dust if not quickened again by the Lord of life.

The soul of Rome was the Pope. He had now left her. True, it was to his own great detriment as well as hers. But Rome had too frequently forced him to drink deep of the cup of bitterness. The Pope's influence on the city from his distant home, could be only very little, if any at all. It was only when some extraordinary circumstance turned up, that Rome would show any signs of life, and even that, but for a moment during this period.

In the second year of the Avignon exile, in May 1308, the Romans were suddenly startled by the cry of "fire" through the city. The Lateran Basilica was in flames. Spite of all that could be done, this, the mother Church of Christendom was fearfully wasted. The fire was regarded as a just visitation of God in punishment of the city's sins. To this succeeded earthquakes and devouring plagues. Of these we have some meagre accounts, and then all is still again in Roman history. Rome sinks back into obscurity and is only casually heard of on occasions of quarrels between princes or noble houses. The city is gradually dying away. No man's life or property, especially if a stranger, is safe within her walls. The Pope, indeed, sent legates to the city to see to the reparation of the Basilica, as well as to the restoration of order. But the former only was effected. Legates were also sent from Avignon to the ill-omened coronation of the Kaiser this year. The history of Rome all this time is merely the lifeless, uninteresting story of a little provincial town. The king of Naples is vice-gerent of the Pope. He keeps his own vice-gerent again in Rome. The one and the other lets the city go piecemeal to the dust. The Romans felt how fallen was their condition during the years 1330–35. They sent repeated embassies to the Pope earnestly praying his return. They solemnly renounced all those rights they had been quarreling for, or had wrested, in the course of time, from the Church. The Pope promised to come. He had the Vatican and its gardens set in order. But the king of France refused to allow his return. Robert, king of Naples, was appointed vice-gerent again. Everything was going to wreck and ruin in the city. The untenanted palaces were mouldering to decay. The churches were ill-cared for and deserted. The city walls were crumbling down on all sides. The Romans themselves carried on a base traffic with the monumental and artistic ruins of their city. Marble columns, church sills, and other cut-stone work, such as tombstones and the like, were carried off and sold for a trifle in Naples. Petrarch tells us how indignant he was to witness this. His indignation is just what an old Roman in the days of Augustus would have felt at the sight. The poet calls on the Pope to have pity on the dying city of the Tiber. He compares Rome to an aged matron with gray hair, wasted countenance, and tattered garments, yet with lofty mien and a noble pride derived from the glorious reminiscences of her youth.

During this period Rome is but the bloody theatre of the ignoble faction fights between the Orsini and the Colonna. Wherever any of the opposite parties chanced to meet, there weapons were drawn and blood spilled. Murder followed murder, and by new murders were these again revenged. "I know not," says Petrarch, "for what evil deed of this people, or by what decree of heaven, or by what fate, or by what power of the stars it is, that peace is banished from this place. The shepherd goes forth armed, to defend his flock not from wolves but from robbers. The husbandman is clad in armor and drives his oxen not with the switch but with the lance. There is here no safety, no rest, no humanity. All breathes of war and hate, and the deeds that are daily done are such as one might expect of the spirits of darkness." The tone running through these letters of the poet, shows the coexistence or rather the permeation of the two ideas in Rome,—the Christian and the heathen. The heathen idea was kept under but never uprooted by Christianity. It waxed strong at this period and for a time prevailed over the Christian in the minds of men. This is the explanation of the follies that ensued.

We have already remarked that all through the middle ages some indistinct reminiscences of ancient paganism acted with more or less influence on the political ideas of the Romans. They were now in a perfect fever on the subject. Theirs was not that enthusiasm that inspired the ablest and best men of this and the following age with a love of classical antiquity. It was a childish silliness that found vent in empty declamation about the heroism of the Romans, the triumphs of the Capitol, the Senate and the Republic. The chief movers in this farce were men of no learning or ability, but demagogues who could inflame the populace by their stirring and pompous, though commonplace harangues. The mass of the people who had everything to lose and nothing to gain by the quarrels of the nobility, seized eagerly on this idea of the Republic. A republic would free them from the oppression of the nobles, make them their own proper rulers, and what not? In Cola di Rienzi, a man taken from their midst was found the very person fitted to carry out their ideas. Cola appeared in Rome unexpectedly as a meteor, and, like a meteor, disappeared again. But that he arose at all, is a remarkable sign of the times. Rome felt she owed all she was to the Popes. Impatient at this, she wished to be something of herself, and at the same time not to do without the spiritual chief of Christendom who was hers by reason of her supernatural destiny. It was a wild endeavor.

Rome created to herself a phantom. The thing appeared for a moment on the stage as the ghost of ancient Rome, furiously declaiming and gesticulating. It threatened to overthrow everything in the city and throughout all Italy. It took men so by surprise, they believed it real. Even outside of Italy, its fantastic movements turned some of the best heads. But it soon appeared that it was all a mockery, a vision of the brain. The windy machine swelled and swelled and swelled, and then burst and disappeared as a soap-bubble.

Cola di Rienzi, the son of a tavern-keeper in the city, had found an opportunity to learn a little Latin. He read Livy, Sallust and Valerius Maximus. Of an ardent and enthusiastic turn of mind, the young man fancied Rome ought to be in his day, what she was in the times described by those writers. "Where are those heroic Romans?" he would often cry, "Oh! that I could see such days in Rome again!" Cola's brother mingled in those tumults that were then so common in Rome. He was murdered in a fray. Cola sought to bring the murderer to justice, but failed. This embittered Rienzi against the existing state of things in Rome. He became a notary public and was one of an embassy sent in 1344 to Clement VI. to persuade him to return to Rome. Rienzi was spokesman on the occasion. He denounced the Roman nobility in violent terms. He accused them of being the cause of all the miseries of Rome, and laid to their account the insecurity of life in the city. He went on in fiery language to denounce them to the Pope as guilty of all the evil deeds that were daily committed in Rome. "The city," he said, "was a scene of hopeless desolation, and it was the nobles made it so." The Pope listened with gracious attention to his words, and dismissed the embassy with the most encouraging assurances. On his return to the city, Cola began at once to work the Romans up and fire them with his own ideas. On the nobility, he could have no influence. By them he was simply despised. He caused a large painting to be made representing a ship caught in a storm at sea. The vessel was seen tossing in the tremendous waves and driven in hopeless plight without mast or rudder before the fury of the tempest. Aboard this ship is a weeping female, clad in widow's weeds, with hair dishevelled and tossing loosely to the winds. Over the figure of this female were the words: "Such is Rome." This picture Rienzi had hung up on the walls of the senate house. In the churches, on the streets, on the public squares, Cola delivered glowing speeches. He dwelt on the fallen fortunes of the city and recounted the glories of yore. The barons at first looked on the whole as a harmless farce. They amused themselves listening to the ready and eloquent speaker. But soon another tale was told. The commoner whom they derided, Cola di Rienzi, was suddenly become lord and master of Rome. The secret of Cola's power was the lively and keen sense he had of the sad condition of affairs, and his honest and enthusiastic wish to apply a remedy. But how to mend matters was the question. Cola fancied it could best be done, by adopting that form of republican government which existed in Rome at the heyday of its power, and of which he had read in the classic authors. But even his knowledge of republican institutions as of classical literature in general, was only very meagre. From what he had read of the quarrels between the people and the patricians, he seized on the idea of a popular tribune. To stand as such at the head of a new Roman Republic, was the ambition of Rienzi. This was the end he had in view and towards its attainment, every nerve was strained. This revolution of Rienzi took the fantastic shape it did, owing to the strange admixture of ancient and modern ideas by which it was produced.

IX.
ROME A REPUBLIC.

RIENZI wielded an immense influence over the populace. On Whitsunday, 1347, he called a meeting of the citizens on the Capitol. There, he was to publish the fundamental laws of the new Republic. Between midnight and morning he assisted at thirty votive masses of the Holy Ghost. He then marched bareheaded out of the church, preceded by three banners carried in solemn procession. On the first, which was of red velvet trimmed with gold, was a figure of Rome seated on a chair supported by two lions. The figure held in one hand a terrestrial globe, in the other, the palm of victory. The second was white. On this was represented St. Paul bearing the sword and having on his head the crown of justice. On the third banner was Peter, holding the two keys, to which Rienzi attached the signification of peace and harmony. From the high steps of the Capitol, Cola addressed the thousands below. He explained the principles of the new Republic, wherein the security of the citizens against the tyranny of the nobility was particularly provided for. The people received his propositions with the wildest enthusiasm. That he might more effectually carry the new system into operation, they clothed

Rienzi with dictatorial powers. His official title was Tribune and Saviour of Rome.

The news of these proceedings at first spread alarm in the court at Avignon. But the arrival of an embassy from the city on the part of Rienzi, allayed all uneasiness. The awakening passion for the study of classical antiquity at the time was such that Rienzi really found a great many mistaken admirers among the educated classes. Influenced by this current opinion, the Pope actually nominated the Tribune governor of Rome. How entirely, even men of note misunderstood the transactions at Rome is evident from the writings of Petrarch. The poet was himself the great head of the classical revival. He grows enthusiastic over the new republican Rome. 'He already sees her, in spirit, queen of the universe once more. He hails the Tribune as a third Brutus, a Camillus, a second Romulus. "Thou standest," he writes addressing Rienzi, "thou standest on a lofty watch tower, and thy fame is without limits to-day, and will endure forever." In the new Republic, he sees a thorough change in the state, the beginning of the golden era, another feature in the history of the world. With phrases chosen out of Livy the poet bids success to the renowned City of the Seven Hills.

The Pope named a commission of four cardinals to see to the restoration of public order in Rome. For though he let Rienzi go on, the city could not be governed by stilted phraseology drawn from the classics. Nor had Petrarch any more practical sense than the bombastic Tribune. He thought the prelates named by the Pope to see to Roman affairs, wholly unfit for the task, owing to their deficiency in classical lore. He fancied it incumbent on him as a patriot, to direct them. He accordingly published two memorials. The maxims of policy prescribed therein are simply transcribed from Livy. The main question discussed is, whether nobles alone, or burghers also, should be elected to the highest offices in the state. "If you would remedy the evils of Rome," he writes, "you must set before your eyes the example of those times in which the city was raised from nothing to the very stars." They must hold on to the title of Roman Republic. With Petrarch no other name is greater or more glorious. The Roman populace of his day was no whit different from the *"Populus Romanus"* of Livy. The nobles are the "foreign tyrants." This nobility abused the long suffering of the people and treated them as "Cimbrian or Carthaginian prisoners." At best, the nobility should be barely tolerated. For this opinion, he appeals to a decision of Manlius Torquatus. To the nobility of the Papal States, he then holds up as models for their imitation, Valerius Publicola, Cincinnatus, Fabricius and Curius. He then launches forth again in praise of the Roman people and extols them to the skies. "How or why should it be," he asks, "that such a people, once masters of the world, who from yonder Capitol defied the Senones, who beheld kings trailed to their cars of triumph, who listened to the prayers of ambassadors sent from foreign lands to propitiate them, who bent or broke the stiff necks of their own ambitious fellow-citizens,—why," he enthusiastically demands, "should not such a people have a share in the government?"

Petrarch in this, as in all else he wrote touching practical life, must be content with having his vivid imagination admired and his literary merits duly appreciated. It was not the airy imagination of the brilliant poet that could introduce into the States of the Church any good practical measures of government. For this was required the good strong common sense of such men as Cardinal Albornoz. The Cardinal was as devoted to letters as Petrarch, but he was not the mere sentimental visionary which the poet was.

The poor crazy man who announced the new Roman Republic to the world, used at first in all his official acts, to couple the name of the Pope's vicar, the bishop of Orvieto, with his own. But as fortune continued to smile brighter and brighter on him, he concluded after a while to set even this formality aside and act simply and solely as Tribune of Rome.

His history, his haughty bearing that amounted almost to insanity, and his violent death, are all too well known to need any further mention here. Day by day, he became more and more venturesome. He assumed additional titles and honors, and he bestowed, as something great, these silly distinctions on his demented followers. This was all the more ridiculous, as he had issued an order forbidding the use of the word "sir" in speaking of any one save the Pope, to wit, that the Romans may acknowledge no superior except the Lord and his Vicar on earth. He also prohibited by law the use of any armorial bearings by the nobility. No escutcheons were tolerated save those of the Pope and the Roman people. Yet he himself assumed a coat of arms, bearing the ensigns of the two keys and the S. P. Q. R. Rienzi, in fact, was intoxicated with success. Seeing himself raised to an eminence that overtopped his highest hopes, he fancied his elevation was due not to circumstances, but to his own personal ability. He wished to have the whole drama of Roman story played over again, with this only exception, that one man—Cola di Rienzi—was always to be head of the Republic. The difficulty was, how or where, or in what capacity, to place himself, as such, in a republic moulded after that of early Rome.

Rienzi with his republic was to do a world of good. Under his government, the good should be protected and the wicked punished. Even and impartial justice should be dealt out to all. The poor should be relieved and assistance given to the widow and the orphan. Sinners should be converted and brought into the bosom of the Church. All variance between husband and wife should cease, and family discord be no longer heard of. Such were some of the many blessings which the Tribune promised should flow from the new regime. But by what means or measures he was to compass these glorious results, does not appear. Of these Cola gave the world no clue. Nor do we see Rienzi making a single, serious effort to realize his fair promises. Towards the end of his career, he seemed even wholly to lose sight of the noble purposes he once had in view. So completely did he get wrapt up in the silly vanity engendered by his ambition, that he forgot all else. He fell from his dizzy height, and the mighty Tribune was found to have been only a crazy, ranting school-boy.

During the Avignon period, not only Rome, but every other part of the Papal States repeatedly strove either one by one, or all together, to throw off the rule of a foreign Pope. When the Pope was about to return, the States of the Church had to be formed anew. This task was achieved by that great statesman and general, Cardinal Albornoz. A whole century however elapsed after the Pope's return to Rome, ere the Papal States in their full extent were admitted into the European family of nations. The necessity of these states to assure the freedom of the Holy Father was now better known than ever. It was admitted and proclaimed by the council of Basle.

X.
THE CITY WITHOUT THE POPE.

THE population fast dwindled away. It went as low as 17,000. Empty houses were everywhere toppling down. Grass grew in the streets. Vegetables were planted in the Forum. Hogs and cattle were fed in another portion of the city which has since been known as the Cow-Field—Campo Vaccino. Besides the monastery we mentioned in a former chapter, the senate-house still stood on the Capitol. But it was so fallen to neglect that it was not even fit for a private family to dwell in. The rest of that hill whose name resounded through the world, was covered with bushes and briars. A number of goats usually ranged its sides picking their scanty food from the briars. The Capitol was hence called the Goat-Hill—Monte Caprino.

In a petition addressed to Gregory XI. by the Roman citizens in the year 1376 they say: "Return, good father, for the appearance of this city, once so great, once so honored through the whole earth, is altered to that degree that no one could recognize in it the holy city and the capital of Christendom. Our most celebrated and holy temples, those monuments of the piety of the great Constantine in which the chief bishops of the Church, clothed in the robes of their dignity, took possession of the chair of the

Apostles, stand now deserted, are left without respect or care, and threaten to crumble down completely. The Cardinal's churches, those sacred spots in which repose the remains of so many holy martyrs, are deserted too by those who from them hold their titles and honors, and who are thereby pledged to see to their condition. The churches are all going entirely to wreck. The walls are broken in several places, and the windows and doors fallen in, so that cattle range through them and browse off the very sanctuary."

Petrarch after his own fashion describes the same desolation and lays the fault at the door of the citizens themselves. The letter is addressed to Rienzi but intended for the public eye. "They (the nobility) for whom you have so often shed your blood, whom you have maintained with your own substance and raised to princely positions by denying yourselves the pleasures of life,—these men do not deem you worthy of freedom.... Nor do they blush but rather boast openly of their crimes. They are not restrained by any feeling of tenderness and respect for their native land. Her holy temples, they plunder with godless rapacity, her garrisoned forts, they strip and demolish. Ruthless wretches that they are, it would seem, they want to wreak their vengeance on the very brick and stone of the city. When either by force or neglect those ancient palaces crumble down in which great men once dwelt, when those triumphal arches which were erected in their honor are demolished, these men do not hesitate to drive a reckless, disgraceful traffic on the ruins thereof and win base lucre from the desolation of the city. And now, oh! shame of all shames! those marble columns of yours and that rich stone-work of your churches around which people of all lands lately stood in wondering admiration, and the rich chiselled work and monuments erected to the dead 'neath which rest the honored ashes of your ancestors—to say nothing else, must go to ornament that murky Naples. Thus even the very ruins which might still witness so eloquently to your ancient glories disappear. And you, in the face of these few robbers who pillage Rome as if it were an enemy's city, you are mute not only as slaves, but as if you were so many dumb beasts, while the garments of your common mother are so shamelessly torn away."

This state of desolation continued during the whole of the period of the great schism. "You can turn in no direction," says an eye-witness, "without meeting some splendid relic of ancient art either stuck into a wall as a common worthless stone, or lying neglected in a gutter." The broken fragments of beautiful marble and porphyry columns lay scattered on the streets, and many of those that are now admired, were then set up as studs to support some wretched hovel or rudely constructed stable. Another writer of the day complains: "We have to witness many things that sadden our sojourn in Rome. In several places we find only grape vines, where we formerly admired splendid palaces. Their highly wrought free-stone is now burned to make chalk." The youthful poet who was afterwards Pope

Pius II., bewails the same thing in verse, of which the following may be accepted as a translation:

> "Thy ruins, o Rome, to see, is indeed a pleasure to me;
> In the relics of ancient days, thy former glory is writ;
> But the beautiful stone from its place in the olden wall,
> Thy people doth burn to lime, and all for pitiful gain."

Some of the ancient temples were actually torn down to serve as quarries, and others converted into lime-kilns. Such in particular was the case with the temple of Vespasian. The cut-stone work was used as door-posts, steps and foundation stones. Some, of delicate workmanship, was used as paling, and more of it might be met with converted into water-troughs. "Greater is Rome's desolation to-day," says Poggio, "than it was under the terrible Marius: more complete her destruction, than that of Carthage. No city ever witnessed such a reverse of fortune. The utter destruction that has come upon her has robbed her of all beauty and comeliness, and there she lies now on earth, a disfigured and sightless ruin like the corpse of a once powerful giant."

Ruins are, indeed, an old thing in Rome; older even than the city of Romulus. He built on the sevenfold ruins of the Septimontium, that is, on the ruins of the seven little cities that formerly capped each of the seven hills. The history of this queen city of the world begins with ruin as does the history of the human race, and Rome could at all times exhibit not only the improvements of each century of her existence, but also the ruins of each of those centuries. But that scene of awful, woful wreck, ruin and desolation that she now presented, was reserved for popeless Christian Rome. It looked as if those words addressed to Saint Benedict were fulfilled: "Rome shall be shattered by thunder and lightning and tempest, and so sink in a mass of ruin."

We, in Germany, look on that period as the worst in our history, when Germany was without a kaiser. For the Romans it was when Rome was without a Pope. Later on we find Rome on three other occasions without the Pope. Under Pius VI., Rome was an appendage of the French Republic; under Pius VII., it was capital of a department of the Empire; and under Pius IX., it was a republic of Mazzinian assasins.

XI.
THE ROMAN REPUBLIC AT THE CLOSE OF THE XVIII. CENTURY.

On the 15th of February, 1798, a party of revolutionists assembled in the Forum under the protection of the French army. There, in presence of generals Murat and Cervini, three notaries had to draw up an instrument wherein it was announced that the rule of the Popes was forever at an end, and that the Romans thereupon claimed, as they were entitled to, the inalienable rights of man. The party then betook themselves to the Capitol with general Berthier as triumphator. The tree of freedom was set up. Berthier, decorated with a laurel wreath, mounted the rostrum and said: "The sons of France are come with the olive of peace to raise up these altars to freedom, the foundations of which were laid by the first Brutus." French commissioners then gave the new Roman Republic a constitution moulded upon that of France. The French titles were translated into those of the ancient Roman Republic. The Council of Ancients was called the Senate, and they had Tribunes, Consuls, etc., etc.

Pius VI., now a venerable old man of four score years, remained meanwhile in the city although he could have easily made his escape. When arrested he begged in the most urgent manner to be allowed to die in Rome. "One can die anywhere," rudely replied the officer in the most contemptuous tones. The venerable old man was sent a prisoner to France, where he sunk under the weight of his griefs, and expired at Valence on the 29th of August, 1799. "The last Pope is dead!" shouted the infidels and heretics throughout the world.

Thus were those little peaceful states and their peaceful prince fallen upon, without any provocation, by the French. The quiet march of progress was arrested and the States of the Church had to undergo more indignities, oppression and hardship than fell to the lot of any other portion of Europe even in those frightful years. Pius VI. had already by the treaty of Tolentino ceded the two patrimonies of Avignon and Venaissin to France. He had also given up the three legations of Ravenna, Ferrara and Romagna, and bound himself in the sum of thirty million francs besides. The Directory proposed terms of a concordat which the Pope had to reject. He was then to be deprived of all. But Bonaparte admonished them to be prudent. "The Popes' power," he tells them, "was still immense in Italy. I am convinced," he writes, "that Rome, once we have got possession of the provinces of Ferrara, Boulogna and the Romagna, with the thirty millions of francs to be paid us, can no longer hold up. The whole machine must fall to pieces of itself." Rome was then robbed of her finest monuments of art and letters. Palaces and churches had to give up their most costly objects. Eighty statues, a hundred paintings, and five hundred manuscripts, all at the choice of the commissioners, were torn from the doomed city. Besides this, heavy supplies for the army and employees were levied upon the Romans, and large and shameless contributions in specie were extorted. Churches were plundered: bells were melted down for their metal, and those objects which could not be carried off or converted into money on the spot, were barbarously injured and destroyed. The richest families were reduced to beggary by the enormous and arbitrary exactions of those in power. The loss which the city and churches suffered, is inconceivable. Of three thousand pieces of sculpture that were known to have been taken away from the Papal States by the French, only twenty-two were afterwards returned. Twenty of the finest antiques remained in the Paris museum, thirty thousand ancient coins and medals, together with the Vatican collection of precious stones, were likewise retained. Among the manuscripts that were afterwards returned, was the ancient uncial code of Virgil. It was magnificently bound when it came back but, the characters were cut into in the binding in two different places.

This time the Romans held aloof from the revolution, although the French had counted on their co-operation. It was the sans-culotte themselves with a parcel of Italian ragamuffins whom they had taken under their protection, that proclaimed the short-lived Republic. General Berthier after his inglorious entry into the city, writes to Bonaparte:— " I am in Rome, and see only pale consternation on every face:—no sign of freedom. Only one single patriot has presented himself to me. He offered to set two thousand galley-slaves free. You can easily judge how I received his proposition, etc." On the departure of the French, the Republic died out of itself.

Pius VI., on his death-bed at Valence, ordered that the ring he wore on his finger should be handed to his successor. He saw no human probability of his having any successor. But he was fully confident that the See of Peter should not remain vacant. The ring, that relic of his trials and his virtues was joyfully received by another and as great a Pius.

XII.
ROME, CAPITAL OF THE TIBER-DEPARTMENT.

The meek Pius VII., the noble prince of peace, and silent sufferer, had, for eight long years, held out immoveable against the all-powerful Napoleon. The insatiable ambition of Bonaparte coveted those little states which were barely sufficient to insure the Pope's independence. The struggle between Napoleon and Pius affords one of the most instructing lessons of history. Craft, flattery and persuasion, threats and rude violence are all alike ineffectual. The humble Vicar of Christ has only the fear of God before his eyes, and in his soul there is only one spring of action, duty. For man, he cares nothing. His lamb-like patience is unconquerable and his irate and mighty opponent had, at length, to have recourse to force.

In this moment of extreme danger to Rome, the Pope and his people were of one mind and one heart. The Romans looked up to their venerable father with feelings of tender affection. His steady constancy was strengthened by their prayers and his soul was buoyed up by their cordial devotion and encouragement. He knew what awaited him. He sought strength in constant prayer at the tomb of the Prince of the Apostles to whom his divine Master had said: "Strengthen thy brethren."

On the 17th of May, 1809, a decree was issued by the emperor, bearing: "The States of the Pope are united with the French empire." The French province of Rome was divided into the Trasimene and Tiber Departments. This wholesale robbery was sought to be defended in the following manner: "Whereas Charlemagne, emperor of the French, our illustrious predecessor, has given the bishops of Rome several small territories under the title of a fief for the better assurance of peace to his subjects, without, however, allowing Rome to cease to be a part of his empire; and, whereas, the union of the two powers hath ever since that time been the fruitful source of contentions, and is so still.... therefore have we felt ourselves obliged, etc."

On the 10th of June, while the French cannon announced the end of the States of the Church, the bull of excommunication against the authors of this robbery was also read in full daylight during the vesper service in the chief church of the city. This created immense excitement among the French who were then in Rome. The Roman people stood bravely by their chief. But like him, they had to submit to force. The most distinguished of the nobility sent the Pope their thanks for the step he had taken, and the entire populace expressed their determination strictly to observe the dispositions of the bull, by avoiding all intercourse with those under the ban. This was on Sunday. Next day not a single one of the state or city employees was at his post. They had rather sacrifice all than serve the new government. Even the porters and errand-boys of the custom house, the street scavengers and such like, were not to be found at their several places. It was only two days afterwards that the Pope issued an instruction prescribing the manner in which individuals should conduct themselves towards the French authorities. Such noble conduct on the part of a population wholly unarmed in presence of those conquerors before whom all Europe shuddered at the time, is certainly worthy of all praise. The cardinals, the prelates, and the entire Roman clergy, as cardinal Pacca testifies, imitated the bold example of the Pope, thus leading the way for the people.

General Miollis, military prefect of the new French province, wreaked his fury on those cardinals who had held any state offices. He drove them into exile or had them imprisoned like felons without any regard to justice or common decency. The Pope was urged formally to renounce the temporal power. The gentle Pius was found in his day of trial to possess the fortitude of a hero. He proved worthy of his high office,—worthy of the greatest of his predecessors. General Radet waited on him to say he had orders to arrest him if he persisted in his unwillingness to renounce all right to govern the States of the Church. When the general apologetically added that the duty was a very unwelcome one to himself but his oath to the Emperor left him no alternative but to perform it, the Pope replied in quiet dignity: "General, if you fancy yourself obliged to carry out such orders in virtue of your oath to the Emperor, you can well comprehend how much more strongly We must feel bound to uphold the rights of the Holy See, to do which, so many oaths compel Us. We cannot therefore renounce what does not belong to Us. The temporal sovereignty of the States of the Church belongs to the entire Catholic world. We are but the administrator. The Emperor may put Us to death, may have Us hacked into a thousand pieces. But, bring Us to do this, never." Pius VII., as is known, was led off and cast into prison. Rome was then five years without a Pope.

It was not altogether for the sake of the little territory of the States of the Church, which, at that time, would be only a bagatelle to Napoleon, that he had recourse to this extreme. It was because he was enraged at the independence which the Pope displayed when he refused at the Emperor's bidding to declare war on England and close his ports to English vessels. To this arbitrary command, Pius only answered that, as Spiritual Father of all, he could make war on no nation. Besides, Napoleon wanted of all things else, to destroy that very spiritual independence of the Pope. He wished to make the spiritual power subject to himself, to be able to direct its actions and use it as a tool for the furtherance of his views of conquest. He acknowledges this in the memoirs composed at St. Helena: "I did not doubt," he says, "but I could, in one way or another, acquire control over this Pope, and then, see what an influence that must have given me!" He wished to have the Papal court at Paris, and make it a Franco-imperial institution which should give him a standing influence in all Catholic nations. But he failed to effect it. The imprisoned Pope, who was according to Napoleon's own testimony, as meek as a lamb, and as sweet as an angel, could never be brought to his views or induced to co-operate with the imperial policy. But the history of these five years demonstrates even to evidence what a superhuman degree of firmness that pope must possess to do his duty, who may ever happen to fall into the hands of king or kaiser, or be, in any way, subject to their power. If he act up to his duty, it will be a constant miracle. The sovereignty of the Papal States secures his independence, and so, fidelity to his trust in the natural course of things. By a miracle of history, the very punishment inflicted on Pius, fell afterwards to the lot of the haughty conqueror, who thus sought to destroy forever the independence of the Popes.

That crime committed on the person of Christ's vicar was the turning point in Napoleon's fortunes. The giant that was never overcome, is suddenly struck blind. He was wounded in Spain, stunned in Russia, felled at Leipsic, disabled at Waterloo, and then chained to a lonely rock in mid ocean, to make bitter atonement for the deed.

The conduct of the Romans during the French domination corresponded to what the illustrious prisoner of the emperor had witnessed with his own eyes previous to the captivity. This noble conduct was already sufficiently known from history. But latterly we have had another testimony on the subject. The private secretary of Prince Napoleon has lately published a volume of diplomatical documents which are to verify what the prince was pleased to say in the senate, as to the evils of the Pontifical government. The secretary was certainly very unfortunate in his choice of documents. Those he selected go to prove the very contrary of what he intended. He supplies the very best matter for our purpose. Among many others, he cites the dispatches of one Ortoli. This Ortoli was an agent of the French government in Rome, at the time, the States of the Church were incorporated into the Empire. In a dispatch dated May 24, 1810, Ortoli writes: "We gain very little here with the native Italians. Most of them will be for a long time yet of very dubious fealty, and unfit to serve the Emperor wherever enthusiasm and unwavering fidelity are required."

Neither the agent who penned the dispatch, nor Prince Napoleon's secretary who has now given it to the public, seemed to have any idea of the praise therein awarded to the sterling loyalty and patriotism of the Roman people. In another dispatch, he says of the clergy: "The priests are still at their old lunes. Should we insist on their taking the oath, it is easy to see that all, save perhaps a very few, would refuse." Other documents are produced in proof of the bad government of the States of the Church. But the private secretary of Prince Napoleon, M. Hubaine, seems to forget that all this throws discredit not on the Popes, but on the French who then governed the Roman States. These dispatches are taken from the official archives that cover the four years from 1809 to 1813.

Pius VII. had seen to his states and to their capital as a good and prudent prince 'till he was carried into captivity. For testimony of this, we need only refer to the French writers themselves of that period. When the Holy Father came in 1804 to the coronation of Napoleon in Paris, he was received enthusiastically by the different state corporations. The speaker of the corps legislatif, M. Fabre, who was still a strong republican addressed the Pontiff in the most eloquent and flattering terms as regards the government of the States of the Church. "If we consider your Holiness," he says, "as a temporal prince, we here find only additional motives for our praise and admiration. Your household and personal expenses are but those of a private individual. Your Holiness seeks that true glory which consists not in the dazzle and pomp of an expensive court, but in a wise and judicious administration. Agriculture, trade, the fine arts, are in the most flourishing condition in the Roman States. Taxation is not arbitrary as of old, but is subject to just regulations and equally distributed among all." The orator then passed in review the regulations of the different departments of the Papal government, and eulogistically alluded to the completion of the land-registration in the Agro-Romano, the premiums awarded to encourage agricultural improvement, the perfection in all that related to coinage, the introduction of cotton factories, the draining of the Pontine marches, etc., etc." He concludes: "The city of Rome notwithstanding all she has suffered is still the home of the fine arts. Your Holiness has caused further explorations to be made in Ostia. Every masterpiece of art that could be purchased was procured. The triumphal arch of Septimius Severus stands out again to view, the Capatoline street is discovered, etc., etc." Many of these improvements disappeared under the rule of the French.

By a decree of March 10, 1814, Napoleon who had now experienced a decisive reverse of fortune, gave back the States of the Church to the Pope. Pius VII. left his prison in Savona. Under a strong escort of French troops, he was conducted to the Taro where the victorious Austrians and Neapolitans were encamped. A colonel of an Austrian regiment Radetzky had a bridge thrown across the stream for the passage of the Holy Father. As soon as the Pope set foot on Italian soil, Radetzky cast himself in joy at his feet and exclaimed: "Holy Father, thou art free and treadest once more the free soil of thy native land." At this moment, the French troops on one side of the stream, and the allies on the other, all knelt to receive together the blessing of the Common Father of the faithful. The Pope entered Rome on the 24th of May. Arrived at the Milvine bridge, the horses were unharnessed, silken ropes were attached to the carriage, and the Holy Father was drawn triumphantly through the Porto del Populo to St. Peter's by twenty-four young men of the best families in Rome.

The countless multitude of the people welcomed back their king and High Priest with every demonstration of joy, and all knelt to receive from his holy hands the blessing which he devoutly imparted in the name and by the power of the Eternal King and High Priest. This day—24th of May—has since taken its place in the list of festivals, and is consecrated to the Mother of God, under the title of Help of Christians—*Auxilium Christianorum*. This title given Mary, is a beautiful counterpart to that given her fourteen hundred years before by Pope Sylvester on the ceasing of the persecution—*Gaudium Christianorum*, Joy of Christians. Mary is indeed the peace and the help of Christians, and she is especially the heavenly guardian of the successor of St. Peter and his See.

During the years of the Pope's imprisonment, the population of Rome did not exceed a hundred and twenty thousand. On his return, it soon ran up to a hundred and eighty thousand. These figures may possibly be a little under or over the mark, but only a little. We have to quote from memory, having no statistics at hand.

XIII.
THE REPUBLIC OF ASSASSINATION.

ROME underwent the same misfortune under Pius IX. that she did forty, and fifty years previously under Pius VI. and Pius VII. She was again without a pope. This time it was no conquering despot dealt Rome the blow. It was given by Italian hands, and, heavens! such hands! The Genoese Mazzini, the panegyrist of political assassins, and that scatter-brained fanatic of Nice, Garibaldi, are the captains of the band. The modern political ranter is not very unlike his crazy predecessor Cola di Rienzi, save that our Nicene is the sworn and deadly foe of the Church of God, which with all his faults, the Roman Tribune was not. This Garabaldi was the arm, Mazzini the head of the last Roman Republic. The whole fiasco only brought unspeakable misery on Rome, and shame and contempt upon Italy.

Pius IX. was elected on the 17th of June, 1846. His first act as temporal ruler of the States of the Church was the publication of a great plenary indulgence, such an indulgence as a king can grant, —a general amnesty to political offenders and the remission of all penalties incurred for political crimes—*il Perdono.* Unlike spiritual indulgences, contrition and confession, amendment and satisfaction were not required for the gaining of this. Nevertheless the paternal prince who granted it must have naturally expected the thanks and gratitude of those who were benefitted thereby. But alas! as regards most of them, he was bitterly disappointed. Those pardoned were utterly unworthy such an act of grace. Still the act itself remains a precious jewel in the crown of glory that encircles the brow of the magnanimous King-Priest. After this followed, at brief intervals, measures of the highest utility to the people. The different provinces were represented in the government, a militia was organized, the city senate and municipal council were restored. We know no case of a prince bestowing of his own free will, *motu proprio*, so many political rights and privileges on his subjects. Pius IX. thought he could place his subjects on as good a political footing as those of any other prince. Accordingly he entrusted them with all those political privileges enjoyed by the people under other governments.

The senate and representatives were to form the government. The house of representatives was that situated as we before remarked on the Capitol. The senate and city council waited on the new Pope at the Quirinal palace, to thank him in the people's name and receive his blessing ere they commenced their labors. Their president, Cardinal Altieri, thus expressed himself on the occasion: "From this far-famed Quirinal, we now go to yon other famous hill, on which the fate of nations was so often discussed and decided. We rejoice that the warlike character of the Capitol has been changed into one of peace. There we shall enter that ancient temple," (for the celebration of the votive mass), "where we shall be reminded of the prophetic voice that announced the new era of peace and happiness to mankind." From this address, we see how vivid are the reminiscences of ancient times to this day in Rome, and also, how the city's olden monuments have become in modern Rome so many eloquent tongues proclaiming Christianity to the world.

All the noble and truly patriotic Italians paid their respectful homage to the new Pope. Pius IX. was hailed on all sides with the most enthusiastic demonstrations. But the picture had its dark side too. By his unreserved amnesty, the Holy Father had cleared the way for the professional anarchists. They crowded into Rome. Those who before had to stay abroad and conduct their nefarious revolutionary schemes from a distance, now pitched their headquarters under the very shadow of the Vatican. Meantime Pius IX. with his natural goodness of heart and simplicity of purpose pursued the work of reform. But these men wanted no reform. Revolution was their aim. The mischief of their presence was soon felt. The militia were brought under their influence. Whenever the maintenance of order or the protection of the government required its services, the soldiers evinced hesitation, unwillingness, inactivity. It was plain they could not be relied on in an emergency. While all this was going on in the dark, the very men who were in league with Mazzini were most demonstrative in their devotion to Pius IX., and most prodigal in his praises for the measures he had inaugurated. The great object was to wheedle the honest-hearted Pius into a war with Austria, and get him at the head of an Italian uprising against the German. The opposition of the Pope to taking any part in such a war, determined the opposite party to deprive him of all power. A revolutionary ministry under Mamiani was forced on him. He appointed the able duke Rossi, formerly French ambassador in Rome, his prime minister. There was still every appearance that, with the assistance of Rossi, he could restore order again and curb the already wide-spread revolutionary spirit. Seeing this, the leaders of the revolution, Mazzini, Sterbini, Ciceruacchio, and others doomed Rossi to death as the man whose energy was likely to defeat their plans.

Rossi was to open parliament on the 15th of November. Hours in advance, the lobbies and vestibules, and the streets which led to the senate-house, were all thronged. The ministeral carriage drew up at the foot of the steps. There the crowd and the jam was designedly closer. The minister stepped from his carriage and moved to ascend the steps. He was received with shouts and hisses. A rude blow was struck him. As Rossi turned to see whence the blow had come, an assassin on the other side, plunged a double-edged dagger into his neck. The blow was aimed by a practised hand. An artery was opened and the Pope's minister lay dying in his gore at the threshold of that palace in which measures for the constitutional liberties of the citizens were about to be introduced. Most of those around were revolutionists. Of course, no one arrested the assassin. Many, if not all of themselves had, at one time or another, been guilty of a similar crime. The members who had already assembled in the house, were constrained by the banditti to proceed with the discussion of their paragraphs as though nothing had occurred. The scenes of horror that now followed in the "Eternal City," we forbear describing. The Vatican was stormed. The Pope narrowly escaped and fled to Gaeta. All power fell into the hands of Mazzini and Garibaldi. 'Twere hard to exaggerate the disorders that ensued. Farini, a radical writer of the day, tells us that the parliament huddled together under Mazzini was composed of notorious characters and stupid boobies who knew absolutely nothing of political affairs. The murderer of Rossi received a grand ovation. The instrument of the deed, *il sacro pugnale*, was exhibited publicly in the streets of Rome, and the event celebrated in hymns and chansons in the evenings. One of the numerous assassins took up his quarters in St. Callisto. When the Republic fell, no less than fifteen bodies, mostly of Romans, priests or religious, were found in the adjoining garden. The inhuman wretch had murdered his victims for mere pastime.

The "Eternal City" was now a den of thieves. It was a grand reservoir of crime. All the ruffians not only of Italy but also of other lands hurried to Rome. Most of the churches were plundered and nearly all profaned. The bells were melted down and converted into a worthless currency. On Eastersunday Mazzini came forward on the Loggie whence the Pope on that morning was wont to impart his benediction to the entire world—*urbi et orbi*—and proclaimed Rome a republic. Robbing, stealing, burglary, forgery,—with these, Mazzini's republic commenced, and such, too, was the order of the day, till it was at an end. The French arrived and easily took the city by storm from Garibaldi and his crew.

What intensifies our disgust at this republic is, that assassination was formally sanctioned by these republicans and adopted into their system of government. In the most reckless and desperate characters, we generally find some spark of humanity remaining which, even when all other moral sentiment is gone, makes them shrink from deliberately taking a human life. What then could be thought of these modern "Roman republicans" who could with brutal indifference practise cold-blooded and systematic assassination? They must have already descended to the lowest conceivable depths of moral turpitude.

During the sixty-nine days of the Republic, the inhabitants of Rome and the States of the Church were forced to drink the hot chalice of the revolution to the bitter dregs. Foreign ruffians roamed over the country, terrified and abused the inhabitants, burned, robbed and wasted. Deeds of infamy were perpetrated without number as without remorse: fear and terror reigned throughout. Whoever could at all, betook themselves to flight on the approach of the miscreants calling themselves the

"Republic" and "republicans." This was a Roman Republic without Romans, and indeed without republicans, for history tells only of banditti, assassins and robbers.

Thus the argument, that Rome, if not the city of St. Peter, is simply nothing, and can be nothing, is affirmed in every epoch of history, and we have seen it, even in our own day, again receive the most signal confirmation.

XIV.

THE TWO HUNDRED AND FIFTY-EIGHTH PETER AND HIS ROME.

NONE of the two hundred and fifty-seven successors of the Prince of the Apostles bore the name of Peter. These men were of different conditions in life, different extraction, different nationalities, different characters. Yet in this long line of rulers, a unity that almost amounts to identity is observable, so that, taking them all together, Peter's successors may be said to be one person with himself.

As there is nothing in the world's history greater than the Catholic Church, so there is nothing grander or more exalted in the Church than the Papacy. The Papacy has had a historical development replete with ever varying and astonishing vicissitudes. But in all the divers phases of its history, that same law which governs the life of the Church, the law of growth, of steady development from within, is also unmistakably apparent in the Papacy. It is this which gives it its strength, which makes it imperishable. To all outward appearance this wonderful institution appears under the most unpropitious circumstances. It is no strong monarchy grounded on family inheritance where the father opens the way to the son, where each king feels that his blood will beat in the pulse of each of his successors through long generations. Neither is it a powerful aristocracy, nor a senate, transmitting their powers as well as their names to their heirs, and so, by handing down the family traditions as well as the family name, making the generations of ages as but one man. The Papacy is an elective monarchy. The term of each reign is generally only a very few years. The throne is often vacant, and consequently it is naturally the most unstable form of government. Behold that long line of old men many of whom reign only a few months or even a few days. And yet, Peter reigns in each of his successors, and his spirit animates them still, after a lapse of eighteen hundred years. Whence this phenomenon? It is not surely in the natural order of things. It comes of the power and protection of God on Whose word the Papacy is grounded. Christ tested Peter's faith, and then appointed him in His own stead. He made him the corner-stone of His Church, gave him the keys of the kingdom of heaven, and entrusted him with power to bind and to loose. Peter's love was first proved, and then the Saviour conferred on him the supreme power in His Church, by these words: "Feed My sheep, feed My lambs." The entire edifice of the Church arose through the working of the Holy Ghost upon the foundation stone thus laid. These few words: "Feed My lambs, feed My sheep" come ringing down through time as if constantly uttered by the voice of God. They are pregnant with great results, and though verified each instant, can only receive their complete fulness in the lapse of ages. He who uttered them is the Logos the

Word of God made man. His words quickeneth unto life. His Spirit disposeth all things sweetly, and abides with, and watches in a particular manner over the Church. Hence the words which her divine Founder addressed to Peter when He made him the foundation of His Church are now equally applicable, as if again addressed in person by Christ Himself to St. Peter's successor, Pius IX. The latter is, as Peter was, the Church's visible head. He is the central point round which all must revolve; he has charge of the flocks and herds, as Peter had, and to him, as to Peter, is given the command: "Strengthen thy brethren."

And gloriously does Pio Nono, the loved shepherd of our souls, fulfil his task. As was written on the basis of that statue of St. Peter of which we spoke page : "Standing firm on that rock divinely hewn, *he* staggers not," but strengthens his brethren all round. In his noble and saintly soul is the living faith of a world, the faith of the entire human race.

Peter was not what he was, for his own sake. It was for the sake of the Church, for the good of the entire human race, he was invested with the primatial prerogatives.

In like manner, his successors are not to be considered as individual men, but as belonging to the whole Church and holding a trust for her sake. In something of the same light must we view that city in which Peter fixed his see, thereby making it the capital of Christendom. It is no longer a city like other cities existing for its own sake and for its immediate surrounding territory. Through Peter and his successors it was indued with a character of universality. Rome is not in figure, but in very deed, the queen city of the world, the capital of Christendom. In its existence lies a significance and a scope, all divine. In Rome, stone and marble, with the reminiscences annexed to them, have become tablets or landmarks in the region of the spiritual world. There, one feels a connexion between the place and the events of history, such as is nowhere else perceived. Everything stands in close relation with the imperishable Church of God. The city itself is bound up forever with the Papacy. All that strikes the eye speaks of Christ and of his Church. Of Rome, in a particular manner, may the words of the Apostle be used: "The invisible things of God are understood by the things that are made." Stone and marble, at Rome, are not mere stone and marble. There, those works of art chiselled into such beauty, do not simply proclaim the fame of the artist, who chiselled them. To him who hath eyes to see, they speak of great deeds entailing eternal consequences wrought here by God's servants,—they speak of the eternal truths of salvation. God laid His own divine impression on this city, when His hand imparting an everlasting blessing rested on the head of the Prince of the Apostles.

And what has the Peter of our day done for this city? As regards spiritual things he is constantly pouring upon her the fulness of grace. He loves the Romans, as a father does his children. He adorns their city with new and magnificent monuments of faith, of charity, of letters, art and industry. He allows them as large a measure of municipal freedom as any city can boast of. He, the Priest-King, gives the laity not merely a small share of political power, not merely half but, a full nine-tenths. He, the sublime representative of authority upon earth, gives to all earthly things, as far as they are good, and harmless, their fullest sphere of action.

This close relation of the Pope with the City, since it first sprung into being, is the normal condition of Rome. It is necessary for the general well-being of the entire Church, and is absolutely indispensable for the freedom of the Pope. As we remarked, it was often sorely disturbed in the course of centuries. But it was never disturbed, without the Church and civil society becoming thereby the sufferers. The Church came out triumphantly from these trials. She was only purified by them. Not so, European society. The existence of the latter is not guaranteed by any divine promise. That was often shivered to its very base, and seemed at times actually in its death-struggle. When the Pope was forcibly driven out of Rome and flung into a prison, there, was the Church, too: "*Ubi Petrus, ibi Ecclesia.*" It matters little whether his prison be a fortified town like Gaeta, or be a dungeon in Valence, Savona, or Jerusalem. The rock on which the Church is built, is found wherever Peter is. Round him are gathered the faithful of the entire Church. Their prayers and petitions ascend to the throne of God for their imprisoned High-Priest. God hears their prayers and restores them Pius as he did Peter of old. But woe to him who puts forth his hand against that rock. He shall be dashed to pieces, and he on whom that rock descends shall be crushed to atoms. It were almost worth while to subjoin hereto the work of Lactantius: "*De mortibus persecutorum,*" for the special information of all present and future persecutors of the Popes. Lactantius does not chronicle many deeds of blood in his book, but portrays the dark windings of deceit and treachery towards the Roman pontiffs, which caused them to suffer a martyrdom of soul at the hands of wily diplomatists.

How comes it, then, that this Rome so essentially the city of St. Peter's successor,—his, by every right and title, his, in a way that no other city can be said to belong to king or kaiser, prince or commonwealth— how comes his possession of this city to be questioned in our times? Why is it that all means are resorted to, to rob him of this patrimony? Heathenism which history tells us was cast long since out of this city, is now returned with seven other unclean spirits still worse than itself, and is striving to regain possession of its former seat of empire. Every nerve is strained to undermine the Papacy, which is the foundation of the Church, and thereby to bring ruin on the entire structure. What forces but those impelled by the powers of darkness, could stand so arrayed against the Church? The war is between Heathenism and Christianity. What men hate in the Pope, what maddens the revolutionists against him, is not that he is a temporal prince or head of a good or bad government. They hate Peter in him, they hate the "Rock," they hate him as the head of the Catholic Church which has warred against, and consequently been hated by, heathenism for the last eighteen hundred years. Let the Pope act fatherly or despotically towards his subjects, let the Church be mild or severe, refined or barbarous, learned or unlearned—the Pope is still the Vicar of Christ, the Church is the divine work of his hands. In effect, it is against Christ, that the war carried on against Pope or Church, is waged. Heathenism is the one great eternal enemy of Christ and Christ's Church. At different periods it but assumed different names and appearances. To-day it is the revolution—the revolution whether on the throne, in the streets, or in the dens of thieves and midnight assassins.

It is now a hundred years since a man but too famous, and as fascinating as he was famous,—a man whose genius had all the dazzle and brillancy of a fallen spirit, and whose heart like such spirit was devoid of all moral feeling, and completely hardened in depravity,—since Voltaire in frantic hate of Christ raised the cry against that Church shouting "crush the wanton"—"*Ecrasez l'infame.*" Voltaire's followers have ever since echoed and still repeat the blasphemer's "*Ecrasez.*" Their modes of attack are various but it is all one and the same crusade against the Church of Christ. Voltaire's friend, Frederic II., wrote him at the time: "The easy conquest of the Papal States may likewise be looked forward to. This done, the Pallium is ours, and the history of the Papacy is over. For no potentate in Europe would be willing to acknowledge the subject of another power, as the Vicar of Christ. All will then, each for his own states, set up a patriarch.... By and by, each ruler will break from that unity of the Church, and we shall then have in each kingdom a native religion as well as a native tongue."

Bravo! Frederic. This is plain speaking, and none of Voltaire's followers whose name is legion could set forth the ends and aims of their machinations in rounder and clearer terms. But your words are sufficient. They go straight to the mark. All else is moonshine. Italian nationality, popular voting, deliverance of the Romans:—this is all gammon. It can only be intended to deceive and ensnare the simple. "Rome or death:" this, the cry of heathenism against the Catholic Church. It is war, and war to the knife, between the two. All we hear, means this. It is only Garibaldi and Mazzini who openly espouse the doctrines of Frederic II. and Voltaire, the one in the language of a barbarous freebooter, the other as the gloomy dark mysterious bandit.

And these views accord exactly with the ideas of the day. Men's minds are as it were infected with a pest. The one star which lit up the moral world is lost sight of. While these men deliberately turn their backs upon this light, they would persuade us they are called upon to lead mankind to the highest pinnacle of perfection. They must renovate all things, create new principles of government, alter the existing social relations, and give a different direction to the course of events. In a word they must shape the future of the world. History treads too slowly for them. They cannot wait till things develop in the natural way and into their natural and proper proportions. *They* must create all. In this vain striving, they waste their energies and their lives, and too often find, that the events they labored so earnestly to bring about for certain ends, stand like giants on their own path. They then discover that, after working their whole lives long, they have but effected the very contrary of what they wished. It is only he who serves God, that can be sure he is not laboring in vain. This is as true of the ruler of empires as it is of the simple peasant. The man who does this, understands that every act and effort of his life, should be directed to the one end of developing in his being the germs of that higher life which the grace of God originally planted in his soul. This, the man feels and acknowledges with humility. In all he does, in all he undertakes, this is his guiding star. Such the elementary principle—simple and natural that a child may seize it—which guides the successor of St. Peter. This was the natural foundation of their supernatural wisdom; this the secret of their prudence in earthly things, a prudence that might put to shame the ablest and keenest diplomatists. The policy of him whom we now venerate in the chair of Peter, is equally simple. Pius IX. does not force events or unnaturally strive to shape them. He accepts what God sends in the natural course of things and endeavors according to the dictates of Christian wisdom, to make the best of circumstances. His only wish is to diffuse heavenly light, and life, and love, through all, and at the same time to advance as far as may be, the temporal welfare of his subjects. He is ever ready to grant them the fullest measure of political power they are capable of using, and prefers to entrust them rather with too much, than too little political liberty. His Romans love him in return as a Father, and they reverence him as their king-priest. It is only a few of the most worthless among them who side with his enemies. The lessons of the past have not been lost on them. The Roman nobility last year afforded us a proof of what we assert. A committee has been formed exclusively from the ranks of the nobility, for the defence of the Holy See. The names of all the first families in Rome are enrolled on the list. A special committee waited on the Holy Father and informed him that the Roman nobility placed their lives and lands, as needs be, at his disposal. Pius IX. was touched by this display of loyalty. He accepted the offer, and replied that he would be proud to avail himself of the same, should it ever become needful. This was the last news that the year 1866 brought us from Rome.

Such the relation of the present successor of St. Peter to his City, to his States, to the world. His toils and his thoughts must indeed be directed to the events of the day, but eternity is what he holds chiefly in view. He knows that no immediate control over the things of this world was entrusted to him. It may happen that in some catastrophe brought on by man's rashness or short-sighted ambition, St. Peter's successor may be seized on and bound, as Peter was of yore, and led whither he would not. But such danger will not blanch Pio Nono or cause him to vacillate. His faith is firm.

He is not to be shaken. Storms may arise. Let them. Pio's eye is steadily fixed on a polar star that never sets, and neither tempest nor sunshine can turn him a single point from the steady course of duty.

Many years ago—the clouds on the political horizon were then slowly darkening—the writer of these lines was one day overtaken by a sudden storm in the neighborhood of the Borgo. He hastened to the shelter of the colonade before St. Peter's and entered the Church. While there waiting for the storm to blow over, he knelt at the marble balustrade that surrounds the tomb of the Apostle. After a little, the weather cleared up. The sun burst through the heavy clouds. The light streamed into the lofty dome overhead, and suddenly lit up, as if by magic, those prophetic words running round the frieze of the dome, giving them the appearance of a crown of glory over the tomb: "THOU ART PETER, AND UPON THIS ROCK I WILL BUILD MY CHURCH, AND I SHALL GIVE TO THEE THE KEYS OF THE KINGDOM OF HEAVEN."

Many of those who visit Rome are struck with the effect thus produced by the sunshine on the inside of the dome. It is one of those many beauties in that wondrous work that were never calculated on by the architect. These grand gilded letters thus gorgeously lit up over the tomb of St. Peter, telling us that the Church is built upon a rock, inspire the soul with confidence. As we remarked in a former place, one sees, as it were, and feels all through Rome, the immediate presence of God and the working of the Holy Spirit in the Church. This it is perhaps which gives Christ's Vicar that rock-like firmness whereby he stands forth a noble model to the bishops of the world, strengthening them and all his children in the faith.

Those words of Christ that we have quoted assure the Church that, in spite of all the storms that may roar around her, in spite of all the powers of hell, she is to last to the consummation of the world. The linking of her foundation stone with that city of eternal fame is clearly the work of God. Shall that connection be severed? Although reason may not give the answer to this question as clearly as it is given by the voice of faith, yet even for the former there is the long period of eighteen hundred years to judge by. We may argue of the future from the past. Judging from this we dare boldly say that, notwithstanding all the efforts of his enemies, the Pope will, in the future, as in the past, continue at Rome and thence forever govern the Church of Christ. This confidence seems to animate the Peter of our day, the imperturbable Pius. In the moment of his greatest danger he calmly summons the bishops of the entire world to Rome to that spot of the old unchangeable "DEUS TERMINUS," to witness the ideal as well as the actual union of the Pope with his city, and to renew, together with their august chief, the old landmark, which Peter eighteen hundred years ago set up in Roman soil.

END.

www.ingramcontent.com/pod-product-compliance
Lightning Source LLC
Chambersburg PA
CBHW020828230426
43666CB00007B/1143